LIVING BEYOND SELF DOUBT

Conquer Insecurity, Boost Self Confidence, Improve Decision Making, and Reclaim Your Self Esteem

SOM BATHLA

www.sombathla.com

Your Free Gift Bundle

As a token of my thanks for taking out time to read my book, I would like to offer you a gift pack:

Click and Download your Free Gift Bundle Below

You can also grab your FREE GIFT BUNDLE through this below URL:

http://sombathla.com/freegiftbundle

More Books by Som Bathla

[The Power of Self Discipline](#)

[The Science of High Performance](#)

[The Way to Lasting Success](#)

[The Mindful Mind](#)

[Conquer Your Fear Of Failure](#)

[The Mindset Makeover](#)

[Living Beyond Self Doubt](#)

[Focus Mastery](#)

[Just Get It Done](#)

You may also visit my all books together at *<http://sombathla.com/amazon>*

CONTENTS:

PART I: INTRODUCTION 6

Why Are You Here? 6

You Support Your Self-Doubts 12

You Don't Want It So Badly Yet 13

What Will This Book Teach You? 22

PART II: HOW DID YOU END UP HERE? 28

Take a Look Back 28

Now Here Comes Your Fault! 37

PART III: YOU ARE NOT ALONE 45

Get A Bit Relaxed 45

You Can Do Anything 52

Language is Your Instruction Tool 58

PART IV: 3 MOST IMPORTANT QUESTIONS YOU SHOULD ANSWER FIRST 61

PART V: 13 PROVEN WAYS TO CONQUER SELF DOUBTS AND REINVENT A NEW YOU 79

1. Doubt your Self-Doubt 81

2. Beware of Your Well Wishers 89

3: Get insulated from "What will People Think" Virus *100*

4: The Magic of Certainty Of Outcome *108*

5: Disrupt Your Mind *116*

6. Do It Scared *125*

7. Start with End in Mind *138*

8. Action is Your Master Key *146*

9. Use Lack of Knowledge as Positive Trigger ... *154*

10. Never Blame Again *164*

11. Seek Help relentlessly *176*

12. Be Your Own Thought Commando. *187*

13. Create Your New Surround System *194*

Final Words... .... **204**

PART I: INTRODUCTION

*****

Why Are You Here?

So you were just surfing the internet and somehow stumbled on this book page on Amazon. You looked at 'To the Point' book title, promising sub-title and also the flashy book cover with bright colors would have caught your eyes. Instantly, the next step you took was to buy the book.

Is it so?

Nope, I guess it is not that straightforward!

There probably are some deep burning questions inside you. Maybe you clearly know, or somehow, these thoughts are running in your sub-conscious mind.

And one more point, and I will be too blunt with you. Most of us would not want others to know that we are reading a book with such a title; "Living Beyond Self-Doubt." The other title could have been "How to Improve Your Self-Confidence or something like "Re-Invent Your Life."

You can sense the difference. The first one shows an ailment, i.e., you have some disease called "Self-doubt." But the other one shows that you have some good elements in you, i.e., "self-confidence," but you simply want to do better.

Some might even go to the extent of thinking that they are already confident and don't need any preaching about increasing their self-confidence. You smell something like burning, right? Yes, this is ego heating up.

But let's come to the point. I have intentionally kept the title straightforward so that it reaches only the right set of people, who acknowledge that they have a feeling of self-doubt in their heads sometimes, or more often. The book also covers the category of people, who despite being confident generally, still acknowledge that often something is nagging in their heads on some aspects of life. This latter set of people are no doubt confident and appear so to the world at large, but in their own hearts and souls, there is something that scares them. There is still something stopping them from their journey from "Good" to "Great," as Jim Collin states in his best-seller book "Good to Great":

> ***"Good is the Enemy of Great"~ Jim Collins***

That's why I have stated that this book is for such people, who acknowledge they suffer from self-doubt which is visible to them (and also often to the outside world). And also, for those people, who are not sure if it is their self-doubt or something else, stopping them from starting their journey from Good To Great.

So, you are here with a thought in your head and a feeling in your heart that you suffer from self-doubt in some manner. Less or more, it is just a matter of degree. But, you acknowledge that there is something, that needs to be worked upon.

Self-doubt simply can be defined **as lack of confidence in oneself and one's abilities.**

So, what is your definition or parameters of self-doubt? What do you consider as self-doubt?

Let me provoke you by suggesting some thoughts or feelings, so it could help you jot down your areas of concern.

    a. You feel like something is lacking in your work life, whenever you

have to deliver some work assignment to your stakeholders.
b. You doubt your capabilities of expressing your work clearly despite knowing and doing your work well.
c. You suffer from anxiety before any of your exams or important events of life, despite the fact that you have twice or thrice prepared for that day.
d. You feel butterflies in your stomach if something new or unrelated to your work comes in your way and you have to deliver the same.
e. You find yourself guilty and incapable of delivering, if you are given something new and start second-guessing your capabilities, despite your past successes.

Does any of this relate to you or would you say this all applies to you?

Be honest with you, please!

You must have heard the advice, to be honest with your doctor, accountant, and lawyer and tell them the complete truth. Why do they advise so?

Obviously! Because, if somehow you are required to reveal those secrets at the later stages, it might adversely affect your health treatment or your tax planning or litigation strategy. But the irony is you don't apply that same honesty to your life questions.

Therefore, you have to be candid about what you think about yourself and your internal thought process while answering these questions, believe me, you will be doing yourself a big favor by being truthful to yourself. Because only then will you be prepared to apply the strategies stated wholeheartedly in this book and get results.

You Support Your Self-Doubts

Often, your mind will try to shift the blame or responsibility for your inner state of doubt to outside circumstances or people around you.

This behavior is, in a way, justifying yourself sitting in a cave and not showing up. You doubt your capabilities in doing something but are trying to pass the buck to something outside.

Take an example:

Assume you have been thinking of public speaking or say any other big thing (as per your circumstances) for quite some time now. But every time you are about to get some opportunity, your self-doubts come in the way and cripple you. Your mind very beautifully engulfs you in a facade of other justifications or arguments to support your self-doubts. These mental statements would look like below:

a. This time is not right, as I am already stuck in ten different assignments, so better to do it sometime later (but you know very well that your "so-called" assignments are normal ongoing things and you can easily manage them).
b. Maybe I need some formal training for public speaking before I could even speak to a gathering of people.
c. Maybe you will think that you are already giving less time to your family or friends and this additional assignment will make you further away from them.
d. Or some other statements like these.

You Don't Want It So Badly Yet

It simply means that you don't want that very thing, as of now.

But except for very few logical reasons (only very few), I bet, everything else is just an excuse. Come on, be honest, you already know that you are lying to yourself. Isn't it true?

You would have heard this very apt quote here;

> ***"If it is important to you, you will find a way. If not, you will find an excuse"* ~ *Anonymous***

So there could be only two reasons. First, that you are doubtful about your abilities and don't want to take the next steps or you don't want the thing as bad, to achieve it now.

Too straightforward, No? And it hurts too, right?

Yes, But the truth always hurts.

Let me tell you a brief story here first.

There was a monk in a village, and he got famous in his surrounding areas due to his teachings about how to live a great life. He was living a blissful life, and people used to come to him for taking his blessings and finding solutions to their problems. A very rich (but not happy) person heard about this monk.

He thought that the monk must have the solution to his problem. So, he went to meet this monk. He asked the monk, "I have everything in life, i.e., money, name, fame, family, social status, pretty much everything. But I am still trying to find my true calling, which gives me the real fulfillment. I am not able to find it, locate it and I don't know how to attain the peace and state of fulfillment which I now see on your face."

The monk listened patiently and then asked the rich man to follow him to his backyard. There was a small pond in the backyard. The monk told the man to get inside the pond, and then he would give the man answers to his deep questions.

The rich man hesitated, but still went inside. The monk sat outside on the bank of the pond. As soon as the rich man entered in the pond, the monk held his head and forced it to be under the water. The man started feeling scuffled, and his throat was choking for want of oxygen. The more force he applied to get out of the water, the more the monk pushed him in the water. Finally, the rich man put his best shot forward and was able to get out of the grip of the monk to come out of the water.

He was furious and almost out of breath. So out of anger, he shouted at the monk, "You wanted to kill me, or what? How do you think such action was necessary to give me answers to my questions?"

The monk said in a very compassionate way, "no, I didn't want to kill you, rather I wanted to see, what you do when you need oxygen to save your life." The rich man said obviously, "one would do anything when it comes to saving one's life."

The Monk smiled and told the man, "Yes, you have given the answers yourself."

> *"When you want wisdom and insight as badly as you want to breathe, it is then you shall have it." Socrates*

The answer to your quest is:

Until you want something so badly, like you want oxygen for your life, you won't be putting your best foot forward. And without that best shot, there is no way that you can get what you want. So, the message from the above story is that you must have a very strong reason to achieve any goals.

Would you think a person would self-doubt himself or herself about getting into a house on fire, if his or her kid is caught in the fire?

No way! Self-doubt only comes in the way, when you don't have a "compelling enough reason" to do something particular.

You Are Here To Find Some Answers

The above story was important to understand first if you are serious about the problem. I wanted you to test out your level of sincerity towards whatever meaningful thing you wanted to achieve.

I wanted you to think again on the below two questions.

    a. Do you often blame your circumstances, the people around, or timing of the things, and hide your self-doubts beneath them?

    b. Do you want that thing on the other side of your self-doubt badly enough and would you want to go to any extent to achieve it?

If you genuinely ponder over these questions and come out with a screaming YES, then you will find this book showering wisdom nuggets upon you with practical, real-life stories and actionable strategies to get you going.

Or You Are Just Looking For Minor Tweaks For Betterment!

Everybody has some doubt in different situations in their day to day affairs. In fact, doubt is a good thing. It comes when you have got something different to do in your regular course of activities, or you are starting out something altogether new, besides what you do. The good part here is that you are exposing yourself to something new and it means you will be learning something new.

There are two kinds of people dealing with anything new in the life. The first set of people are those who embrace those new things and changes and take action on their own. The second set of people are those who just keep staying in their comfort zone longer. Then what happens is that the comfort zone gets tired of such people and they are forced to bring about the changes in their life.

So, the first category of people, who seek for changes, are pushing the trigger themselves and inviting the self-doubts on their own. Obviously, self-doubt comes, when you are unsure of your capacity or capability to do something. This category of people knows that this self-doubt is temporary and it will transition out when they get somewhat familiar with the new thing. They keep moving further.

The second category of people are like those who get thrown into the small water pond (not a life-threatening, but still challenging) by someone so that they could learn swimming. Now they have no choice. They genuinely doubt their capacity to sail through because they have not really, on their own, tried something new. But, after waiting for a long time, now life has shattered them strongly.

You would agree that both sets of people have self-doubts at times, but their approach towards handling is on two extreme sides. One is a proactive approach, and the other is a reactive approach.

This book will present the material, which will further smooth the journey of the first category of people, who seek changes and therefore have to overcome self-doubt. Also, this book will serve as a panacea for those people who are struggling with any changes which life has thrown upon them and now they have to show up and overcome their doubts to proceed further.

So, whether you need to unlearn the past habits and develop a new mindset system for you (for the second category of people), or you simply want some hand-holding steps for further improving the level of confidence, this book will help both sets of people appropriately.

What Will This Book Teach You?

The book is structured as simplistically, as it could be without compromising on the quality of the content. I believe you don't want to be burdened by a full volume thesis explaining your internal psychology, neuroscience in more than five hundred pages of text. I have written this book in such a way that it gives you a basic understanding of what goes on in your head, where it comes from, primes you with the necessary preparation, and then you are directly exposed to the actionable strategies, immediately after reading the relevant chapter.

Though the table of contents will show you what is comprised in the book, still let me give a bit more perspective about how the book is structured.

I. There is always a reason for doing something and always a starting point before you embark upon any journey. Part I is written to help you do some internal assessment of your current situation and will prompt you to figure out what are your real reasons for picking up this book and how you can get the maximum benefit out of this book.

II. Part II allows you to dive deeper and gives you some space for introspection about what specific factors made you think the way you think today. It will prompt you to check which of your actions or inactions are responsible for your current state of affairs. This assessment of your actions is important so that you don't repeat that behavior in future. Also, it goes on to explain how the outside factors have influenced your mindset and where you stand at fault while dealing with your circumstances

III. Part III goes on to explain that your situation is not a unique or peculiar one. It is filled with real-life stories where real people have gone from extreme conditions of life and how they have overcome that difficult period. Not only did they survive, rather they thrived. You will start getting into the frame of mind, by reading the real-life stories and start relating yourself with all those stories.

IV. Part IV is the most important section of the book, as it directly hits upon your psychology and mindset. It is a high-quality stuff, which will trigger your mindset not only to overcome the self-doubt but make you jump out of bed to start learning the actionable strategies stated in the next part.

V. Finally, Part V is the core section of the book, which will invite you to play with your mind, ask tough questions to yourself and learn time-tested and proven strategies which you can start implementing as early as you finish reading the specific strategy inside this book. You will find these strategies with a practical touch clubbing the Author's personal experience of nearly two decades in the corporate world and life in general.

Why Would You Listen To Me?

I have been an avid reader for more than a decade and read multi-dozens of human psychology, mindset development, entrepreneurship, personal development and business-related books. Obviously, I was able to grab lots of wisdom gems and the good part: I experimented most of the stuff in my around two decades of corporate world experience and life in general. So, I have practically tried, tested and implemented most of the strategies in my own life.

I strongly feel that this learning, exposure, and implementation of the great ideas from the top visionaries made me suitably qualified to spread the message around through my writing.

I have written and published multiple books already on the topics of productivity, time management, human psychology, and mindset related aspects. (My previous book "FOCUS MASTERY" has already hit the Amazon bestseller list). I am not trying to brag about it while writing this. But this is only to assure you that this is not a theoretical rhetoric regurgitation of the existing stuff. The message in this book is something which is learned by deliberate reading, exploring and the best part is doing the fusion of others' thoughts with my perspective and life experience to it.

I think this is sufficient explanation. I don't want to use this space more by filling in my intro. Just have a look at my website www.sombathla.com to know more about me.

Moreover, I believe my actions (in the form of words) should speak louder than above words (my introduction).

Okay, get ready to come along with me on the journey.

Come on. Let's start.

*****

PART II: HOW DID YOU END UP HERE?

*****

Take a Look Back

Okay, before we go further, I would like you to turn your head backward. Just look behind you (not physically, but mentally) to help you understand your psychology, so far. Go more back. Keep going back till your childhood, until the ag, when you started remembering things.

You will now start seeing little-blurred memories of your past. You will feel that mental state and the feelings associated with your various life events.

I want you to see with your own internal eyes, what made you think the way you think today. Was it like this since the beginning of your life or had something changed on the way when you were growing up? Try to recollect your childhood days in school. The days when teachers asked you, "What do you want to become when you grow up"?

Try to recall what your answer was?

The real answer, you would have given to your teacher from your heart that day. I guess the answer you had that day did not consider any boundaries or limitation of resources, skill set or anything, which was required to help you become what you wanted to be.

I recall my childhood days and the classroom scene precisely. I used to say I wanted to be a pilot. Don't know why, but somehow, I can connect now, why it was so? In hindsight, looking from where I am here (writing this book), I am somehow connecting the dots. I can say with almost certainty that I always wanted to explore the new things and I had always been looking for new approaches to do anything. That meant never wanting to be settling down, never getting too much in my comfort zone. Being a pilot would have meant the widest possible opportunities, i.e., exploring space, crossing the boundaries of countries. Also, it meant being able to see things from the top. So being a pilot is the right metaphor here, precisely indicating the openness, vastness and willing to explore the uncharted paths.

Now, think about you. What was your answer to your teacher or anyone who would have asked you? Don't say; nobody asked you this question ever. Because being an adult, you and I know that this is one of the most asked questions to any kid.

So, what did you respond? Maybe you wanted to be a teacher, a doctor, an engineer, an artist, a singer or whatever.

These were all clear and clean intentions, without thinking about any conditions or ifs or buts to it. But you know life is not a lonely journey. You stay with your parents, you interact with friends in the school, and you also listen to your teachers. You also visit your parents extended family and interact with them.

What happens next?

And as you grow up, your interactions with the outer world continues to expand more and more. You are with you for a much less amount of time. But you are with the whole world mostly in all your waking hours. You become influenced by the thinking patterns or belief systems of the people in your surrounding environment. What you have been thinking gets diluted with what the world thinks. I mean your short world, which is comprised of a limited number of people around you. You start thinking the way your environment thinks.

You would have heard the below quote already:

> *"You are the average*
> *of five people; you*
> *spend most time with"*
> *~Jim Rohn*

Therefore, your reality is created by the people you most spend time with. Your current reality is massively influenced only by the people around you,

I didn't mean to say that the people always around you will be leading you to a low standard path. History is also filled with examples, where great thought leaders have taken the entire greater thinking from their family and upbringing.

Susan Cain, the author of the best-selling book "Quiet: The Power of Introverts in a World That Can't Stop Talking" talks about her childhood days, where she was always surrounded by a huge number of books. She had grown up in a house full of scholars. Her parents and grandparents had great book libraries in their house. Spending quality time in that house meant to be reading the great non-fiction, uplifting literature, which enhances your level of thinking to a large extent. She describes a wonderful moment in her early teens, when she went to her first summer camp, her suitcase was not stuffed with mementos or forbidden snacks, but with books.

Also, you would be aware of Albert Einstein, the great scientist of our history and known as the father of modern physics. But he was known as slow in learning how to speak. Her mother was summoned to the school by Einstein's school authorities. The school headmaster told that her child was below average intelligence and issued a note to that effect stating that he could not study in the school. The headmaster even expressed his view to her that Einstein would not amount to much in his life.

His mother kept that piece of paper hidden in an iron box and also tightly as a secret in her heart too, till her last breath. She rather told Einstein that he was a super intelligent child, in fact, a genius and therefore, he couldn't school with other normal kids. Einstein believed in his mother's statement and did the amazing stuff in the field of physics, leading to winning a coveted Nobel Prize in Physics. In the later years, when his mother died, Einstein stumbled across that old box and out of his curiosity opened it.. He was shocked beyond his imagination after seeing that note from school and couldn't stop crying, as he realized that his mother had done the best thing by not showing him that letter.

He wondered the magic of beliefs. Had his mother told him the truth about the reason for being expelled from the school, he wouldn't ever have reached such greater heights in his life.

But, not everyone gets so privileged and lucky. Let's talk about those who are not privileged to have such uplifting parents, society or neighborhoods in their lives.

The common statements, which most of the people hear from the surrounding environment are:

- The other person who achieved huge goals had something different in them, how could you do it?
- You don't have that financial situation, or you are not that networked to reach those levels.

- You would have heard- "Stop making a castle in the air, come to the ground. Don't daydream and get back to work."
- The money doesn't grow on the trees etc.
- You don't have that, what it takes.
- And so on.

These statements are generally and very wisely coined as "practical" or the "ground realities", etc. But they have the strong impact of shaping your mindset at an early age. A younger kid is like a wet clay or dirt, and his surrounding environments served the purpose of a potter. Whatever shape the potter gives to the wet dirt or clay, it takes that shape permanently. In my previous book "[The 30-Hour Day](#)", I talked about seven kinds of negative mindsets, which originate due to our upbringing and how you can replace them by taking certain actions. You can get a free chapter of the book on my website at www.sombathla.com, and I promise you will love it.

What is the key lesson here?

The key message here is that starting to doubt our capabilities has its origins in your roots, in your surroundings and upbringing. A child is born full of possibilities. A child is like a seed. Each seed has the potential of becoming a huge tree. But if a seed is not properly sowed, not nurtured in the initial days, not given the right manure of possibilities, not supported with adequate watering, not many seeds become a tree.

You got all your self-doubts from others in your environment.

But should the story end here? Would you say that you (as a seed) are now wasted because of your circumstances? Would you say that nothing is in your control now?

Now Here Comes Your Fault!

If your circumstances have done something wrong with you, does it mean that it has to remain that way for your entire life? Does it mean that you can't change anything now?

If you think that way, then you are at fault.

Having a wrong upbringing never means that there is no hope and it never means that nothing can be done now. There are enough examples in history, with such people, who have overturned their future despite the worst childhood and upbringing.

Let me tell you the story of a girl. She was abused in her childhood and also got raped. She got pregnant at the age of 16. She was mentally tortured and disturbed. Her circumstances were nowhere close to suggesting that she can ever succeed. But she took the responsibility and created an entire media brand in her name.

If you had not been able to guess so far, she is Oprah Winfrey, an African American media personality (net worth > 3 Billion

USD), hosting the Opera Winfrey Show, which is one of the highest rated television talk shows in American Television History. She is the lady, if someone comes on her show, he becomes an overnight celebrity.

Robert Kiosaki, the best-selling author of the famous book "Rich Dad Poor Dad" publicly acknowledges that merely by getting interviewed by Oprah on her show was instrumental in him selling 5 million copies of his book and he was a millionaire overnight.

Less talked about former Indian Prime Minister, Lal Bahadur Shastri, had a very challenging childhood. He used to work during the days and study during the nights. Since his family was poor and had no access to electricity, he used to study below the street lamp. But despite his adverse family and financial conditions, he rose to the highest level of politics in the country and served as second prime minister of India.

I will give one last example of taking responsibility for life about my author friend Zoe Mckey. . She is the best-selling author of dozens of books on human psychology, mindset development (see www.zoemckey.com for details). She publicly acknowledges and tells her life circumstances, in which she was struggling to earn for her food for days. Since shifted from Russia to the United States at the age of 14, she stayed alone and had to undergo so many hardships, which are sufficient for a normal human being to break down easily. The circumstances were enough for self-doubt to creep in, but she didn't succumb to her self-doubt. She was persistent and fully committed to change her life. She is now living a full-time living out of her writing and enjoying the freedom lifestyle, traveling the world.

What do you get from the above stories?

A human being is the only creature gifted by the God with consciousness. A human being has the consciousness to think about, the awareness to judge and distinguish the good from the bad and not only that, take actions to change the life situation.

So, if your circumstances were not favorable, that doesn't mean that your world ends there. A dog can never be blamed for its poor or rich life conditions and is also not expected to change or turnaround its life. But this is not the case with human beings.

Forget about your past. You have still many years left in front of you to change your life, at whatever age you are in your life. You have two types of mindsets, which can govern all your actions. One mindset always thinks about the thought of natural frightening from anything new or which is uncertain and makes you feel insecure. The other is a bolder mindset, which dares to think beyond the clouded negative thinking and into the realms of possibilities. Now the question is which mindset you listen to very often.

You can compare these mindsets to having two different pet animals with you. If you want to make one pet stronger than the other, how would you do it?

Answer is! You will feed one pet more and also with a better diet to make it stronger.

Similarly, if you wish to make your positive side of mindset stronger, you have to start feeding it more by paying more attention to it and by associating it with more positive things in life. In some time, the negative mindset will starve, for want of attention and without any further negativity fed to it.

Anyways, fearful state of mind is not required in this modern and safer age. Our brains were supposed to remain in the state of fear in the primitive ages when the man was staying in jungles, and the fear has an important role to play. You had to always be on your toes, as there was also a real danger of being attacked and killed by some animal in the forest. But in today's world, there is no such threat to the substantial portion of the population living in the almost safe houses with access to most of the basic amenities. The current age does not warrant that kind of fear. It is merely a change in your approach to look at the things differently and take massive positive action.

The purpose of this chapter was to clarify how these self-doubts have crept in your life. You understand that our surrounding environment plays a vital role in shaping our lives. But it also goes on to state that even if the circumstances were not good or in your favor, you should not stop there. There are tons of living examples, where people have even overcome their self-doubt despite being in the most difficult situations in their lives.

With that, let's move to the next chapter, where you will learn that you are not alone in this journey of living a life beyond self-doubt and what you can learn from others on this journey.

*****

PART III: YOU ARE NOT ALONE

******

Get A Bit Relaxed

The heading of this section seems very soothing, right?

It gives you some comfort that you are a part of a bigger crowd. There are other people around you as well, who also doubt themselves. So, it lets you think that you are not an abnormal creature. What a sigh of relief, no?

But, here is the thing.

Everybody suffers from self-doubt at some stage of their life. Some people believe their self-doubts to be true and don't take further actions. Others go beyond their self-doubts and see the light of the possibility even in the unknown ventures.

Now, look at the heading again. YOU ARE NOT ALONE.

It means you are always amongst these two sets of people. But you have to make a choice, a rational choice, a life-changing decision, about on what side you want to be.

Whether you will resign to your life circumstances or whether you will create a marvelous life out of your challenges. Whether you will simply give up, stating the obstacles on your way are stopping you from moving ahead or you will use these obstacles as stepping stones for your next best thing in the life.

You already know, the majority is on the first side, i.e., not taking action and behaving like the victims of life. Because our mind works in such a way that it seeks instant pleasure, avoid pain and wants to feel efficient as quickly as possible. And you know very well that there is no instant pleasure, rather there is a massive pain (mental and emotional), and the mind doesn't immediately feel efficient in doing something which is new for it.

You have to choose, what kind of person do you want to be?

A couple of examples will help you to choose better:

J.K. Rowling, author of the most-selling books in the world "Harry Potter" series, was massively plagued with self-doubt and was rejected countless times, before she became a success. Before publishing her first book, Rowling was living a small apartment in the U.K. with her daughter, unemployed and broke. She had to rely on state benefits just to keep food on the table. She was not sure of what to do with her life. She had gone into the phase, where she was thinking of committing suicide[1]. Then she chose to keep her chin high and persist. The rest is history, one after the other, the Harry Potter book series were selling like hotcakes across the world. Now the net-worth of Rowling is more than 1 billion US dollars.

Take another one.

Ashwin Sanghi is a famous Indian author of the thriller type of fiction books. After his success as a fiction author, he got a thought of writing a non-fiction book. But he was filled with a self-doubt that he has always been a fiction author and whether this venture into non-fiction would adversely affect his career path. He got began to doubt, wondering whether this would disturb his brand image in the eyes of people around.

---

[1] http://www.independent.co.uk/life-style/health-and-families/health-news/j-k-rowling-i-was-near-to-suicide-as-a-struggling-mum-799715.html

But he finally chose to overcome that self-doubt and what happened next? A fantastic book titled "13 Steps to bloody good Luck", a short book filled with tons of success anecdotes on the steps people take and attract the good luck. A recommended read, if you love to learn by examples.

So, you can see that everybody is fearful or skeptical about something in one's life. Even the smartest people sometimes feel self-doubt, but their strength lies in overcoming those doubts, by well-settled principles engraved boldly in their minds.

There is a beautiful saying, which goes like this:

> ***"The brick walls are there for a reason. The brick walls are not there to keep us out. The brick walls are there to give us a***

> ***chance to show how badly we want something." ~ Randy Pausch***

Tony Robbins' below quote helps further to prompt you:

"Model someone who is already successful, because Success Leaves Clues" ~ Tony Robbins

So, you are not alone. If you are willing to look around, you will find tons of other examples, which will help you to move on the success charts much faster. In fact, if you think deeply, your self-doubts beacon you towards you most coveted assets. Let's take it another level ahead.

Before you doubt something, you think about that very thing, right? Why did you think about that thing in the first place? Because you are concerned or care about that thing or it excites you. Note this down and slowly think about it.

My conscience forced me to rewrite the above understanding again because it feels so important to repeat this here (and also because repetition is the mother of learning)

Before you doubt something, you think about that very thing. It means that thing is important to you, you care about it or you are concerned about it. It means that you want to dig deeper into that or achieve that thing.

Are you with me?

You said, Yes! So, let's continue.

Then comes your old negative conditioning of mindset which generates doubts in your head! It shouts loud on your face, "Who are you to do this?" It tells you a dozen reasons that you can't-do it. You have already realized that the thing is really important to you, but you are doubtful if you would be able to achieve it or not. Self -doubt is your barrier to achieve your goals.

A big barrier!

But read the word again. It is called "SELF (means yourself) DOUBT. It is not termed as other's doubt. There is a key in this sentence. It is the word "SELF". So only you are responsible. You, yourself can continue to support that doubt or may choose to overcome that doubt. If something wrong gets accumulated in your head, it is your responsibility to clear that, not your neighbors.

You Can Do Anything

You can do anything, I mean ANYTHING, you desire. I know you understand this. But let me try to deeply fit this into your brain by citing few examples or stories. Because

> ***"Words are how we think; stories are how we link"* ~ *Christina Baldwin***

Colin O Brady, a young man of 31 years got burned in an accident. He was in such a bad condition that his doctors told him that he wouldn't be able to walk normally again in his life. He had enough reasons to self-doubt, due to his severe accident. Moreover, a medically certified doctor was vouching and doubting his capability to walk due to his major accident. But he didn't give up. He determined to climb all the seven topmost mountains in all the seven continents. He became the world's first person to climb the mountain in the shortest period. He explains his worst bodily conditions while climbing the mountain. But he kept on going and going, continuously breaking his self-doubt patterns. If you look at his TED Talk on a

Youtube video, you will get goosebumps straight away. [2].

What do you get out of the above story?

I am not saying that you can fly an airplane tomorrow by merely thinking like this. Yes, you can fly, but maybe after six months or a year of extensive training and practice. You just need to have the mindset to learn and the skill set, and you can do anything.

Success may not come immediately to you, which may again start creating doubts in your head, but that never means that there is some shortcoming or gap in you. Might be you have not taken the right steps at the right time, or there is lack of a right combination of the effective strategies.

You know the sport of Cricket. There is a phrase often used in this game called

---

[2] http://sombathla.com/change-mindset-achieve-anything-colin-obradythe-miraculous-heights-human-potential/

"timing." You have to move the bat at the right time and with the right force at the right place on your bat, and then it is going to be a sixer (getting six scores- i.e., the highest, one can get on one ball).

If you make one element wrong, e.g., you don't apply the right amount of power or force, you may get caught by a fielder near the boundary. Or say you move your bat just a fraction of second before and the ball goes in your wickets and you are out. If you don't hit from the right place from your bat, the ball may go in a different direction, and you may be v out of the game.

> *"Luck Is What Happens When Preparation Meets Opportunity"~ Seneca*

Similarly, life is all about the right timing for different things, and you have to apply the right strategies at the right time. But you don't learn everything in the first go. That's why there is so much importance given to massive action, and that helps you to try so many iterations in the way of doing it. These endless iterations only improve your game, and the seemingly difficult things start appearing relatively manageable to you. Therefore, don't let minor failures come in the way of achieving your goals.

Sometimes the gold is just a few meters down before you think of giving up the idea of digging the soil further.

Also, life is a very difficult subject, and you think that you can get a masters degree without any teacher. All other subjects (other than life) are created by man, and we are quite convinced that we need to put time and efforts to learn those subjects meticulously. But think about your life. God creates it, the most complex curriculum on the planet with different levels of consciousness, thought levels, feelings, emotions and what not.

Also, unlike the human-made things which have the operations manual to operate it, there is no instruction manual or guide on how to operate your life.

Take the example of your car. Your car has an instruction manual. It also states what fuel to put inside, i.e., diesel or petrol. How many times you have to do servicing when to replace the engine oil when to get the batteries checked and replaced. Each and everything so minutely covered. And you also follow them properly. You don't put the wrong fuel in your car. You get it regularly serviced. You get the dirty carburetor cleaned at regular intervals.

But compare this with your life. What do you do with it? You put all kinds of negative thoughts of self-doubt, fear, shame, etc. You put all junk or unhealthy food in your body (no proper energy management of yours). And the result is in front of you, a complicated and lackluster life.

Language is Your Instruction Tool

Words are the language of communication with your mind. You should always choose the right words for being in the peak state of performance. In his book, "Awaken the Giant Within," Tony Robbins has given a complete chapter on what are the right words to be used for different situations of your life, which will give your life a different meaning and thinking arena. There is a big table made comprising around thousand words, with two columns. The left column shows unsupportive words and the right column suggest the word, which should be replaced in place of the negative word, to help you get into the right state of mind.

So you are not alone. There are people around, who have already brought you here and are responsible for all your conditioning full of self-doubt. You can choose to continue to stay with them, and your life will not be changed. You can't go beyond your self-doubt.

But I am sure that since you picked this book "Living Beyond Self-Doubt," so you would choose to go ahead with a different set of people. You are not alone in this journey here as well; it is just a matter of being coachable and learning the newer way of living. Because you have heard an endless number of times already:

> ***"When the student is ready, the teacher will appear"~ Zen Proverb***

The above quote sets the right segue into the next section of the book, which is all about setting your mental machinery ready, not only for clearing your-self doubts, but rather to experience a massive success in whatever area of your lif, you want to improve upon.

Let's gear up to get into the amazing stuff right here in the next section.

PART IV: 3 MOST IMPORTANT QUESTIONS YOU SHOULD ANSWER FIRST

*****

I know you are keen to directly jump into the tactics and tricks to overcome self doubt and start moving the things around in the positive direction. But let me be very candid here. This is not going to be a tonic, which you simply swallow every evening and start experiencing the magic tomorrow morning. Please keep in mind that tactics do very well only if you have the right mindset first of all.

The tactics are mere "How To's," which you can easily find in an endless number of personal development books if you have already read them. But these How To's don't last long, precisely because you don't know have the foundation rightly set up. In other words, you don't have a stable mindset as of now, before you can see any significant results.

Forget about this book or any other topic related to this, before you start the question of "How to" do something, you have to have a clear "Whyto "To" behind that.

We start with How To's with a big bang, but the moment some hurdle or obstacle comes in our way, the motivation fizzles out immediately.

Why is it so?

The reason behind this is very awakening. The author who writes the stuff about how he achieved the success in his life covers all the actions he has taken. The author writes that what strategies or tactics have worked out well for him or her. But it is entirely not possible for the author to let you feel all the emotions or feelings of rejection, fear, and self-doubt, which he or she has gone through while he or she was pursuing that journey. This journey often carries along with it his fair share of sweat and tears faced during the journey. Now the good part is that the strategies or tactics work very well. But before strategies work, you have to be ready to put the work in on a consistent basis. Success in any field or area of your life does not happen overnight it takes time. Often it takes many years before you become an overnight success. And this consistency and the discipline to stay put only comes, if you have some bigger why to stick to. This is only this bigger why, which will keep you moving despite jerks coming on the way.

Take any of your life examples!

Suppose you have to run a marathon or say half marathon or say just 10 kilometers. How does it work? Do you simply get onto the road on the day of the race and simply win the race or for that matter even complete that race?

Even thinking of that seems so stupid, right?

You have to prepare months in advance before that. You have to take care of your diet, so it supports your muscle building. You have to plan your exercise and running regime on a regular basis. You have to develop tons of discipline and self-control. You have to curb your urges to stay longer in the bed in the chilly winter days.

So, do you think, it can simply work based on the strategies or tactics written in the book? It is a much bigger job, my friend. It is not that you have to train your body simply. You have to train your mind. You have to control your thoughts and feeling and emotions arising from your thoughts.

After your persistent preparation for a couple of months, you get ready for that big day. I have personally experienced this, so I know how it feels while preparing (not always very great) and how it feels when you complete the finish line.

The mantra is mindset development and finding your clear "Why" or "compelling reason." With that being clear, you can persistently follow any arduous activity on a regular basis.

I have read the great books: "Slight Edge" by Jeff Olsen and also "Compound Effect" by Darren Hardy, both highly recommended. The significance of daily practice and the persistence is the most significant tool for achieving anything massive.

Therefore, basis my personal experience, which I have learned after listening to the top scholars or Ph.D.'s on the human psychology and reading tons of books, that you have to first work on your Why and the objectives behind any action.

So, to put it precisely, before you start your journey towards overcoming any problem or achieving anything significant, you have to answer these three questions crystal clear as transparent as water.

- A. Have you already stated your **clear objective** or **unshakable why** or **compelling reason** for what you want to do?

- B. Next most important question, one need to ask about is **whether you have crossed your point of no Return**.

C. The third and most important mantra, which you must apply while you are in your journey towards conquering your self-doubts is **to apply the 10X principle**.

Coming to the **first question**, it is worth emphasizing even at the cost of repetition that you must firstly clarify, **why do you want certain things**? Clarifying this one thing is something, which will help you stay put in your journey with dedication and persistence, without requiring any outside motivation.

Clarifying your "Why" or getting to know your "compelling reason" or simply put objective will help you to follow the tactics more vigorously. It will ensure that you are committed to the game plan. And the commitment is something which makes you super resilient. You fall off (often), dust your pants and then keep going. If your son is caught in a fire in a building, no one can ever question or doubt about your commitment to saving him, right?

The next one, i.e., finding or ascertaining your **Point of NO RETURN** (in conjunction with your compelling reason) becomes such an important factor in your progress that it will pull you like crazy. It will work as horse blinders for you, and you will become unstoppable. You will feel the pull and people will be able to see the strength very significantly. That's why you see people around you progressing super-fast and call them as "crazy" (in a praising manner).

But why this is so important?

What happens in your journey towards your massive goals, whenever there is a little gloomy day or something not working out, you immediately start looking backward. You start looking at your past. Whatever activities you would have done in the past, those start appearing to be tolerable or worth returning to (meaning returning to your comfort zone days). This is despite the fact that whenever you had been doing those things in the past, they got to be fussy and you wanted to get out of them badly. Facing difficult times generally makes the people think about olden days, which now seems to be comfortable (but remember these were the only days, which you wanted to avoid).

But let's get to the point. What I mean to say here is or to put it in different words that whenever you are faced with difficult times or things are not moving as per plan, you start thinking of looking backward for other options.

But for the successful and confident people, don't assume that they have not come across any difficult time, rather they had decided deep in their minds there was no question of returning. Once you reach that peak stage of difficult times and when everything appears to be tearing apart, and there is no ray of hope; if in that stage, you are determined you won't be returning, then the magic happens. Then the universe awards you with a gift of ideas or connections, which cross your ways, so beautifully that you couldn't have imagined that way at all. You will start getting all strength, and level of commitment, which is necessary to overcome those hurdles and go beyond that side of the seemingly insurmountable mountain.

Just try to connect this with the below story taken as an extract[3] highlighting the concept of "burning the bridges." Long ago, there was a story of a general who was about to face his greatest and most powerful enemy. One who greatly outnumbered his army. He loaded his soldiers into boats, sailed to the

---

[3] http://elitedaily.com/money/entrepreneurship/burning-bridges-success/

enemy's country, unloaded soldiers and equipment, then gave the order to burn the ships that had carried them.

Addressing his men before the first battle, he said, "You see the boats going up in smoke. That means that we cannot leave these shores alive unless we win! We now have no other choice – we win – or we perish!" They won.

These soldiers didn't have a backup plan. They didn't think to themselves "if anything doesn't work and I am about to die, or we are about to lose we are just going to jump on our ships and go back home to where we are safe and have supper." Instead, they gave themselves no choice but to win and they did so because their backs were up against a wall not up against a road they can run back to. And that is the way you need to see your journey.

This is the power of burning the bridges. There is no looking back. And the only way forward is to look forward and conquer (or die)- no third choice at all.

Now coming to the **third burning question** for massive progress in your life and leaving everything else out of your site. Now you have a compelling reason, and also you have decided your point of no return, there is no reason to go slow. You have to move your pace to 10X of wherever you are in your life.

Dan Sullivan has highly emphasized the important of 10X. He states that When 10X is your measuring yardstick in any area of your life, then obstacles seem dwarfish to you and your entire focus goes to only those factors, which can fasten up your success.

What does 10X mean?

10X means whatever area of improvement, you are choosing in your life, be it your financial, relationship, personal, spiritual or health, you are determined to do ten times better than what you are currently and this entirely shifts your focus and mindset. You are suddenly in a different game. You will start catching or attracting those ideas, which are not available in your normally clouded mindset.

But you would ask, why not go for 2X, which is also double of what you do. But I can bet you, after thinking of 10X concept, 2X will seem dull or boring or not that exciting.

The kind of adrenaline you would feel in your body and mind is beyond explanation. I have personally experienced this, and it keeps your mind so focused that all other things get blurred immediately. You just look at the things, which matter to you most and all other things, which are distractions, just get filtered out without much effort on your part.

Let's summarize how these questions will help you prepare for your journey for conquering your self-doubts.

Firstly, to overcome your self-doubt, you have to do introspection on your real reasons why you want to achieve what you want to achieve. This reason must be so close to your heart that it overpowers all your desires.

Then you have to do a reality check, whether you have reached a point of NO Return. You have to be determined, no matter what, you will stay persistent till you achieve success. Just to add, this Point of No Return is very closely connected with your WHY. If you failed to connect to your real WHY you would miss this point.

Then comes the magical 10X Principle. With a clear why and having established the Point of NO Return, you are on your journey to not only overcome your self-doubts, rather you will be very shortly able to gain such a momentum and surge in your level of confidence, that you will surprise yourself. Now do yourself one favor before you move forward in this book.

Do a journaling exercise. Either open a text document on your computer to type or else adopt the traditional pen and paper approach. Write whatever comes to your mind regarding the above three questions. Be honest with you and do a complete brain dump to help you introspect better when all your thoughts are in front of you. You can effectively handle something, when something is in front of you, right? So, let your thoughts come in front of you on your PC or Mac or your paper. You will be surprised to see what all comes out of your genius head, if you do it with sincerity, as required to handle any life situation.

My friend, I sincerely believe that this section has done the work of shaking you up and now you are ready to learn the proven ways to overcome your self-doubt and embark speedily to your journey towards gaining greater confidence to take massive action towards your goals.

Now, the next section in this book will touch upon actionable tactics, which you must practice for full faith about the effectiveness of these strategies. Even if one reader of this can unshackle himself or herself from the clutches of self-doubts after reading this book, I would feel deeply satisfied. I have personally been there and seen how it feels to be in that stage of self-doubt and inaction. Since I have gone through that bumpy road and personally experienced the intermittent phases of anxiety, stress, and struggle and applied the measures to overcome those, I would want you to be benefitted from my experience. Because:

> *"Life is too short to learn everything from your own mistakes. So learn from others, who have done it already"~ Anonymous*

I am not asking you to trust me blindly. What I wish is that you apply these principles to your own life and see which works better for you and then stick to it. Let the principle of compound effect, i.e., the magic of accumulation of daily practice, work to help you to live beyond your self-doubts and live a life of fulfillment, which comes by achieving your goals.

> *"Big Goals are achieved with*

> ***incremental daily actions"~ Aaron Broyles***

I sincerely hope that this section gives you the required inner motivation to move further. Now, from the next chapter onwards, you will learn the specific actionable tactics, which you can start implementing immediately.

Okay, with that let's move on to the next section.

*****

PART V: 13 PROVEN WAYS TO CONQUER SELF DOUBTS AND REINVENT A NEW YOU

*****

Congratulations, you have made it so far. Your reaching here only shows your sincerity and willingness to get rid of your insecurities, thrash your doubts and start living a life full of possibilities.

In all the previous sections of the book, you have dived deeply into the human psychological aspects behind these self-doubts. You have already seen tons of examples and heard stories, where people from diverse backgrounds and despite all troubles in their way, have not only survived but came out with flying colors.

I believe you have already laid down the solid foundation by doing the necessary groundwork, as recommended in the previous portion of the book. With all that, we will straightforward jump to the proven and actionable strategies in this part.

So, let's get started.

1. Doubt your Self-Doubt

You would have heard "***Iron sharpens the Iron***."

The above proverb aptly applies to this point of the book. Whenever you have some doubt about your capabilities or skills sets or confidence, let your mind to start doubting that self-doubt.

You will ask how it works.

Let's try to understand this by few examples, specifically.

a. You have been given an office assignment, which involves dealing directly with the topmost bosses of your organization.

   b. You have been asked for a writing of an article in your professional or trade journal.

   c. You have got an opportunity to head one of the most important client's meeting and directly deal with a client for the first time in your career.

   d. Or you have been asked to give a speech at an alumni forum of your university.

What happens as a first reaction to these situations with most of the people? You start thinking in your head.

   a. Am I capable enough to handle this important assignment with the topmost officials of the organization?

   b. Do I have the necessary communications skills?

   c. You start feeling a level of anxiety and stress in your head for such things if you are quite starting out.

d. How would I hide my sweat and my trembling hands while standing addressing a large group of people?
e. Who am I to write that article in that established journal or speak in front of a big audience?

You start doubting your capabilities and credentials. These feelings may still arise, even after you have had past successful experiences in your life if you let your mind wander around and get plagued with negativity around.

That is the moment when you have to start cross-questioning. These are the moments, which make or break your destiny. In fact, these occasions can be your life-changing occasions, and for most of your life, you keep on thinking or looking for such opportunities for advancement of your career.

So, in these very moments, you have to do all the mental calculations immediately. But you have to nip these doubts in the bud. You don't allow this to grow into a monster and then trouble you with tons of anxiety and stress.

Start questioning your mind, assuming it is another person standing in front of you, telling you all those sermons (not to take action). Start counter-questioning this other person like this:

   a. So, tell me, what is the special capability or competence with the people who easily do such kind of things. Do they have this inherited or can I also master that stuff?
   b. Does it require something new to learn? Can't I learn that new thing by getting more information, which is easily available to everyone with few clicks of buttons these days?

c. Does it require approaching certain people to help me out? Do I have access to such people? Have I yet tried to reach out to people to help me out?

d. Am I scared of social rejection or bad image, if I unable to complete the tasks? Am I afraid of what people will think if I stammered on the stage and my voice shakes or is cracking? Or I might get faint over the stage (extreme situation).

All these questions will tell only a few things, which successful people do.

a. They do it despite being fearful of the negative outcome- they use courage muscle.

b. They do it without having complete knowledge -- they believe in the below quote:

"Everything is figureoutable: ~Marie Forloe.

 c. They do it despite not having done it in the past- because they know that everything happens for the first time in life and by practice, they can master it. They have the mantra.

> ***"Everything is difficult before it becomes easy, every experience is uncomfortable before it becomes comfortable."***

At the end of the day, it is only the conversation which you have with your mind on an ongoing basis. As I explained in the previous section, your positive and negative mindsets are two different pets. The more you feed the positive mindset by giving the examples of how others have done it, the stronger it will become.

Everybody has doubts. They come because of reasons that there is some lack of information or lack of experience or you have people around you who have tried and not succeeded or never tried, thus not succeeded (and they preach to you about not moving ahead).

But the starting point is to start doubting your self-doubts. YOU have to get down to the cause of each of your self-doubts. You have to introspect then, whether you can overcome these doubts by putting efforts in learning a new skill set, finding the right people to help you out or taking massive action to overcome such doubts.

Sitting on the self-doubt is not helping you, rather it is helping self-doubt to be righteous and stronger. If you allow that, you will make self-doubt a monster difficult to tackle at the later stage. You can always do something in front of self-doubt.

You have to pose the challenging questions in front of your self-doubt. Then, you have to just decide the action strategy at that particular point in time, when self-doubt creeps. You have to decide if you need to learn something new, meet the experienced people or get your head down and keep working on whatever is best at thapointinime.

2. Beware of Your Well Wishers

Sounds too absurd and harsh, right?

Yes, I know it does.

But let me clarify this a bit. You should start with understanding what your definition of well-wisher is? Who are these well-wishers? And probably, you might need to revisit your definition of the term 'well-wisher."

Some of you might be confused. You would say that you already know who your well-wishers are. Then what is this redefining and why it is required?

Okay, let me first hear your general definition of a well-wisher. I guess that you would say the people in your family, your close friends, and relatives, with whom you spend the most time.

Not your fault, most of the population would only define well-wishers like this.

But, my friend, this is a very vague definition. The real definition of the well-wisher is the one who knows what is well (good) for you, means **good for You**. But the prime requirement for that is that such person should also be clear about what your life vision is? What are your priorities? What are your life values?

Tony Robbins in his book "Awaken the Giant Within" clearly stated that every person has different values, as per one he or she lives his or her life. The person will feel blossomed and flourishing, only when he or she can live as per those values, which are a personal compass specific to every individual.

He states there could be different types of values, which different individuals could have their lives. I have listed a few (you may have some other life values as well).

- a. Freedom
- b. Adventure
- c. Security
- d. Certainty
- e. Love
- f. Power
- g. Comfort

Everybody has a different vision of life, based on their life values and everyone follows different role models for that.

Spend few minutes and think about what are your life values? Do some introspection about what is your vision of your life.

- Do you love more of freedom and adventure?
- Do you define security and certainty as your personal values?
- Are you more inspired towards love or does the power puls you towards itself?

You can try to recall a few life instances of yours and try to assess your values basis your internal feelings at that point in time, when you were living those instances. Do you find yourself secure being told to do certain things in a specific way or do you want to enjoy the freedom and power to do the things as you may like? If you want to learn more about learning your values, go and check out this hefty book "Awaken the Giant Within" by Tony Robbins.

Now only if the other person can understand your life values and your vision and then supports you wholeheartedly in achieving that, should be considered as your well-wisher. Others, who don't relate to you can't be stated as your well-wishers.

Now the confusion that happens with most people is due to emotional reasons from these so-called well-wishers, as they would often tell you on your face, "We are your well-wishers, we don't want your bad. We want everything good for you." But if their life values and the vision they had about life don't match with yours, then you will be misguided solely by their values (which will be contrary to your values and vision) and good or bad experiences

Let me take a very personal example.

I have my values of freedom and adventure. I love to keep doing experiments with different things. I love to be doing things at my own pace and do not want to be controlled by another one. I love to move towards unknown and see how the life teaches me differently. On the other hand, my life partner has different life values. Her key values are security and certainty. She wants the things to be pretty much under control. There is no doubt that she loves me and wishes best for me always, but only as per her values. By any means, I can't force my values upon her, unless she is willing to. But assuming, I choose to lead totally as per her values, then it is going to be good for her, but I won't be living a fulfilled life. Therefore, my decision of moving out of a corporate job and being my own boss was a hugely debated topic, as there was a value mismatch. Finally, the good part is that we mutually agreed to give my values the best shot, on the condition that I would be addressing her financial security values in a pre-agreed period.

So, if you have to be very careful while dealing with your well-wishers, you have first to check if there is a value alignment or not. If there is no value alignment, then very often you will keep on doubting yourself, basis the vision and values of others.

How to handle these well-wishers?

Just keep the two things in your mind, and the life will become much easier to sail through:

1. Be clear about what your life values are. You have to test these quite often before determining that. Go and try living as per values, which you think belongs to you. Then check your feelings. If you feel fulfilled in living that way more than often, then go ahead, because these are your real life values.
2. You have to be able to see the clear live examples of your vision. There should be people around you who have lived or are living a life based on the things, which you are visualizing already.

Now you can approach these people differently. If the person is flexible in approach and you think having a clear communication with him or her is something which will clear all the air, simply sit with him or her. Explain your perspective and also listen to him or her. Have a detailed conversation on pro and cons of living your way. If the other person can understand, then treat that person as your well-wisher, as now he or she is with you on your journey.

The other kind of people would be such, who would be inflexible and adamant in their approach. They have a sense of stubbornness and rigidity in their approach. They think that the way they think is the only way to think and there is no other way. Now, listening to such people often will make you feel doubtful about yourself. Also confronting such people will be often more dangerous because then they come in the defending mode.

So how do you handle them?

Don't talk to such people about your values or visions, etc. You can talk about all other things with them except your ambitions or values. You can talk about the fruit or vegetable prices, a chit chat on what's the new movie release or how is the current Government doing or any other unrelated topic like that. I am not joking, you can't talk about your values and life philosophy with such persons, as they don't understand it. Also, the most dangerous part is that you lose your willpower and energy in convincing them, which you could have very well utilized to strengthen your vision.

Secondly, you should use the CTT technique very well with these people. CTT stands for "CHANGE THE TOPIC." If you anticipate some confrontation during some flow of discussions, which may make the environment unfriendly and another person may become too defensive, you should subtly divert the topic to less intensity topic. Don't suddenly start talking about something bizarre (like latest movie release). Remember I said, "subtly" change the topic. Such an approach will help you avoid the emotional outburst or explosion of another person.

So, keep your search for real well-wishers going on. It is not necessary, and you are not always lucky to have them in your home or in your relationships. Make friends with like-minded mentality, who will carry you along on the common vision.

Take utmost care from your "so-called" close well-wishers and you will immediately start improving your way of thinking, as you are not accumulating any other negative thought junk on your mind. By nurturing your mind with positive people and not getting too engaged with your "so-called" well-wishers, you will start winning over your false self-doubts. This will help you to boost your self-confidence and enhance your performance for the better.

If you want to learn more about how to smartly deal with difficult or negative people around you, I have a dedicated full chapter on this topic in my previous book ["Master Your Day Design Your Life,"](#) which you may want to check out.

Okay, now let's move to the next one.

3: Get insulated from "What will People Think" Virus

> *"Don't worry too much about how to explain better to people, they only listen to, whatever they want to" ~ Anonymous*

A substantial majority of the population often start doubting themselves before they do anything different because they get badly stung by their infectious thinking about what people will think.

Let's take an example.

I don't know you, but let's assume for a moment that you work in a decent position in any organization, but you have deep desire to do Stand-Up comedy acts as well. Immediately, your mind will pop-up the negative thoughts about what will people think about you. You might get scared that they might make fun of you for such a decision, as some might think that doing comedy is sub-standard to your decent job. You may get a self-doubt about your identity in the society.

We all know that the human being is a social animal and it cannot stay without a society. The advantage of society is that it gives you a form of connection and belongingness with other human beings. But the associated drawback is that whosoever does something different than the social norm is often criticized, ridiculed or made fun of by the society, at least at the start.

So, the fear of what people will think about you starts creating self doubt in you.

Nobody knows your personal circumstances better than you. People can't get into your head to understand what motivates or drives you. They don't know your vision and your life values.

It is only you, who is into the thick and thin of things, not the other people. It is you, who has to live with your soul, not them. It is you, who has to remain with those feelings of non-fulfillment, not them.

Here is a short but a very effective trick to overcome your fear of what will people think about you.

Next time, you think of doing something different than what you normally do, bring in front of your eyes, a few names and faces, which come to your mind related to those thoughts. How many person's names and faces start appearing in your head. Now make a list of these names on plain paper. Start visualizing the image of these people talking about you and reacting to a particular action which you wanted to take in your life. Try to think about how they will react to it. Would they laugh at you or make fun of you?

Then go one step further. Think about the personal or professional background of each of such person and their values and approach towards life. You already know about your life values and vision towards life (as we talked in the previous chapter in detail already). Now do some more self-talking and introspection.

Do you relate yourself to them or their vision or approach towards the life? Do you think that they are also willing to go the same path as you wish to travel? There are very high chances that if you think that they are laughing at you, based on your action or decisions. Then your life priorities, your vision, and your values don't match with theirs. Therefore, it is amply clear that if you and your people (who come in front of your eyes) are at different paths of life and do the thing differently, then your actions can never be guided by their personal compass.

Moreover, I bet you won't be getting the whole world in front of your eyes when you think about other people. It is generally 5-10 people at the maximum, which you can think of. So, this simple exercise about comparing your life vision and values with those 5-10 people, will help you to strongly conclude that your actions should be solely based on your life vision and values and not on the basis of these limited number of other people.

Let's take a look at this from an outsider perspective as well.

Most of the time, these thoughts about "what will people think" might only be in your head. How can you be sure of what others might think about your action? You feel yourself to be at the center of the universe (everybody thinks that way) and always think that everyone else is thinking about you. It is generally the case that people have very short attention or memory spans. People might think about you for few seconds and then again get switched to some different thoughts and distractions.

How many times do you keep on thinking about the other people at length about their actions? Not too much, right? The same is the case with others too, why would they continue to think about you? They are already stuffed with too much on their own plate about their work, life, career, finance, family, friends, health and what not? Who the hell is sitting out there and always thinking about you? So don't bother too much.

Even if people might be thinking, it may be the case that they are thinking rather very positive things about you. They might even praise your action or boldness of doing certain things or being authentic to your desires, which very few can do in this world.

But regardless of the fact, whether they think good about you or bad about you or they don't think at all about you, how does it matter? So far you are convinced that you are doing your best job towards your own ultimate goal or vision, it is perfectly fine to keep going.

> ***"If you try to make everyone happy, the only person, who would be unhappy, will be you." ~ Anonymous***

Keep one thing in mind; You don't always need permission from people to live your life. Don't worry about the people around and be your own cheerleader in whatever you do.

Most important thing, you need to do is to take utmost care of your thoughts. You don't allow anyone to come to your house and throw garbage or junk material around your home. In the same way, you have to keep your mind clean and never allow anyone to throw the garbage of negative thoughts and doubts into your mind.

Therefore, apply the principles and the practical and tested tactics stated above to get deeper into your self-doubts and completely uproot them from the soil of your mind.

4: The Magic of Certainty Of Outcome

The exact opposite of the phrase "self-doubt" is "certainty of outcome." If you start doubting yourself- it simply means that you have not yet imagined the certainty of outcome in your mind. I would rather say that you have more thoughts of failure and moving back than the certainty of outcome.

Imagine taking your school examination. When you had been preparing for the school examination, did you always have thoughts of failing in the exams and then studied? No! There might have been certain instances when you would have gotten a bit scared. But generally speaking, you always would have studied with a level of certainty of outcome in your head.

And with that feeling, the kind of preparation you have is different. However, if you continuously think of failing the examination, you would not put in any sincere efforts in the first place.

Tony Robbins explains the concept of certainty of outcome and states that if we are certain about the outcome in our minds before we even start the action, our minds guide our actions accordingly.

If you are going for a job interview or if you are producing some creation of your own, would you start with thinking that you are not going to get that job or people will not like your music, video or book? Of course, not!"

If you do that, you would surely be inviting the failure in the first place. A little bit of discomfort or feeling of positive stress is natural because you are doing something other than what you normally do. But overall, you have to start only with a feeling of certainty of positive outcome.

Mind Over Matter

Let's understand this concept of certainty of outcome in your mind through a bit different example.

Anything worthwhile on this planet is first created in the human mind before it has ever taken a physical existence. Take an example of real estate projects:

All of us have seen in the movies many times, and some of us would have seen in the real estate company's office. They have a big table and the complete building layout in the form of blocks. It has all the buildings, flats, garden, roads, moving cars blocks, etc.

How does it look? You get a complete image of the actual building and the residential project by just having a quick look at those blocks. You get a sense of certainty of outcome that the building is going to be ready shortly and it would then look like this.

But even before this wooden block structure, the first origination of idea comes to the human mind, which is an intangible and invisible product. No one can see it except the person, who is imagining it. Then the next work is to put that in the form of big architectural maps with clear measurements of the total areas and how different blocks, buildings and other amenities will look like in that society. Then it follows and presents the protocol in the form of wooden blocks, as stated above. Finally, the real work at the ground starts, with heavy machines, and labor all put to work to create that tangible product in front of you.

I was watching a documentary the other day about the infrastructural developments in Dubai. If you see the multiple skyscrapers buildings in Dubai, some amongst the world's tallest buildings, no one can even imagine now that it was just a barren desert land just two decades ago. We all know that before these huge sky-touching buildings were constructed tangibly, everything was in the mind of human being. Then it came to papers and then to reality.

This is what we call **mind over matter.**

Everybody goes through those stages of self-doubt, skepticism about the future outcome. Everybody has to go through those emotions of fear of failure and defeat while taking the steps towards one's goals.

Is there a choice? Can you avoid those? Unfortunately, no, you have to surpass that.

But How?

You have to empower your emotions of the "certainty of outcome" over your feeling of fear and self-doubt. The more you practice, the easier it will be for you to take action on the things.

To conquer your self-doubt, you have to clearly make a picture of yourself, how you would look or feel like after achieving that particular goal. Imagine your work product in your hands, it could be your new song recording CD, your video, your physical book. Imagine getting that award or accolade for your contribution.

With these feelings of certainty of outcome, you start from the place of strength and I can guarantee you the feeling you have as of now, will be much more empowering. You would be feeling like jumping ahead and taking the quickest action on your goals. You can easily compare this feeling with the one, which you had when you had been thinking from the place of scarcity or self-doubt (which I bet, is very low level of energy.).

Just to give you my personal example again. Before I start writing a book, I imagine the picture of my book available at the online platform and in physical form. I also imagine a badge of Best Seller on my books on the online Amazon platform (My previous Book "FOCUS MASTERY" had hit #1 Amazon Best Seller rank already). I see the final work product in my imagination, and I visualize my feelings about the same. I foresee the cover design in my mind, the title, the tagline, all the chapters, the key message even before starting putting the first word on my laptop. With all that I start a clear outlining in my mind, which follows an outline of the complete book on the paper. Only then it triggers the final writing action. Now I know for a certainty that I have to travel this path from point A (the picture in my mind) to point B (actually hitting the publishing of the book).

Use this concept of mind over matter to your benefit. Add the ingredient of certainty of outcome to this dish. You will slowly and gradually be bidding bye to your all self-doubts. That way, you will have a very sumptuous recipe of success to enjoy lavishly.

Whenever you encounter self-doubt on your way to your biggest of goals, always remember the below quote:

> *"The Loftier the building, deeper must the foundation be laid"*
> *~ Thomas A. Kempis*

5: Disrupt Your Mind

You would have read on various liquid medicines "***Shake Well Before Use***" Why do they recommend this?

So that all the ingredients of the medicine get mixed properly, and you get the maximum benefit from that medicine. The same principle applies to your mind as well. I heard you said, "What?"

Yes, I meant "Shake your mind well before use." Though I meant it more broadly, i.e., disrupt your mind physically as well as psychologically.

Let me try to explain my perspective.

It might sound simple and obvious, but this is powerful. You have to move your body, to shake your mind. The daily routine of exercising your body for 30 minutes is the best strategy to do it. But how this will cure the self-doubt?

Here is the answer. Your self-debt arises from different kinds of fears. This could be fear of failure, fear of rejection from society, fear of financial or reputational loss and so on. This fear can be controlled only through a counter emotion called courage. Just to clarify, courage is not the absence of fear, rather it is taking action, despite being fearful, i.e., taking action in front of fear.

But where from this courage comes?

That's where Tony Robbins (you would have noticed that I am such a big fan of Tony) gives the scientific basis of the origin of courage. Courage comes from moving or exercising your body. If you stretch or force your body to lift weights, it builds not only your body and muscles; it strongly empowers your willpower and determination.

Robbins says, "Do something physical every day, even if it's just five or ten minutes of fast walking a couple of times a day. That tends to replace fear and anger with determination and courage. It can change your identity, your momentum."

I recommend doing the exercise during the morning sessions, if your work or occupation permits. If required, wake up 30 minutes early, but do it in the morning. If not possible, then apply "something is better than nothing," i.e., do it later in the day.

Why morning? Because I said, "Shake well before use." You would definitely want to start your day using your fresh mind to its fullest power first thing in the morning when you have already taken full night's sleep.

Moving your body in the morning will help you build your courage muscle, and you will start winning over your self-doubts in a short period. But as I said in the starting of the book, don't expect magic happening in a day. Rome was not built in a day. It would require consistency and persistence, and within a couple of weeks of regular exercise, you will start feeling the difference in your approach.

I recall my personal experience of past running in the morning before going to work when I was preparing for my 10K marathon run couple of years ago. I was able to focus on my work better, felt happier and courageous to take difficult decisions faster. Currently, I take long walks and do gym for 30 minutes or so before I start my day.

Besides doing regular exercise, you should follow Robin Sharma's message. He recommends weekly massage of your body.

This again shakes your mind differently. It puts you in extreme states of rest and rejuvenation. You get out of your routine thinking pattern and refresh your perspective to look at the things differently. This is another way of disrupting your mind by getting out of regular activities and let the mind wander in a relaxed state of affairs, to generate new ideas for better handling your work.

How to disrupt your mind psychologically?

To overcome your doubts, you have to start building a new set of belief system. Because the existing belief system which you have created by repeating the non-supporting thoughts has already created enough mess in your life. So how do you start?

Start it the smallest way. But the idea is to expose your mind to newer things around. Like the following:

- Try to go to your workplace from a different route on most days, if possible.
- Watch documentary movies on versatile topics be it history, science, technology, adventure, etc.
- Read books on some topics, which you have never read earlier.
- Travel to unique and different places.
- Try to follow a different work approach.
- Have lunch with different people.
- Try street food or different types of restaurants.
- Laugh openly with your or others kids.
- Or try anything different from your routine activities.

I read somewhere that in the olden times, travel was considered the best form of education. Travel teaches you not only in your head, by with your whole body. You go to different places, eat different food, meet people with different cultures, understand different belief systems, etc. This helps you to make distinctions between the things from multiple perspectives.

So, do as many different things as you can do. Because, the idea here is to break the pattern of mind and expose it to an altogether different world. It will simply broaden your mind's horizon. You will capture tons of information while exposing your mind to different scenarios. Your neural pathways build new connections between the old set pattern of beliefs and the new exposure.

T. Harv Eker in his best-selling book, "Secrets of a Millionaire Mind" compares the human mind with a computer and the thoughts and beliefs as different files into the hard disc of the mental computer. His idea is that the output on the computer screen will be the same as the internal files running on the computer. So, he suggests 17 different mental files, which if replaced will help you think like millionaires. The book was written not recently, so you can replace the phrase "Millionaire" with "Billionaire" (the same secrets apply to turn into a billionaire too). I am convinced that Billionaires have traveled their journey from Millionaires, by following this journey only.

This whole disruption process physically and psychologically will show you an entire new world of possibilities. Now you are not relying on the old mental conditioning, which was created by involuntary association with not so uplifting surrounding environment. Through this disruption, your mind comes in association with the newer stuff and the good part is that you have chosen it voluntarily. Nobody is forcing this upon you. When your old self-doubting belief system gets exposed to new pieces of information, you will start gradually reducing your reliance on the outdated belief system. And very soon, it will surprise you that there is no space left for any self-doubts in your mind because all our doubts got generated by staying in the past and living with your dated beliefs only.

So, shake well before use and keep exposing your mind to disruptions.

6. Do It Scared

Okay, let's make this journey bit exciting!

Assume you are in the midst of cold winter season and you have to get out of your bed yet. It is so cold outside that even getting out of the bed seems to be something like going to a battlefield. Your quilt, blanket and the bed which is amazingly warm charged up with your own body heat too. If you are married, then you are with your partner in your bed. Everything is so comfortable, warm, cozy. You can sense the relaxing smile on your face. All in all, a great feeling!

Anyways, somehow you manage to get out of your bed. Then you have served yourself a hot coffee or tea. You are feeling fresh now. Again, all sounds perfect, right?

Yes, so far. Now you are heading over to your bathroom to take a refreshing bath. Just hang on. Here is some minor instruction, you have to follow now. I ask you to open the tap with the cold-water shower.

And yes, here is the main thing. Now just stand straight under the chilled water fountain. What are your thoughts, feelings or emotions? (It is important to check your thoughts if you are doing it for the very first time in your life so far.)

I understand, it immediately gives you an electrifying shiver in your whole body, even if you think of such thoughts. But you have to get under the water shower now.

So, you get up the courage and get under the water. You are terrified. You are breathing like a fast train. The chilled water touches your body, and each pore of your body gets goosebumps raising straight. There is a whole horror scene, and some of you even might scream too. But hang on there for initial 15-30 seconds. You will feel the body settling down, and you will enjoy suddenly start enjoying the chilled water coming to you.

You must try this out. If you are in some hot country, try this with a huge number of ice cubes (which you generally use to make your drinks). (Caution: If you have some existing health problem related to exposure to cold, please consult your expert, before you experiment)

Now what I have just taught you has two specific purposes. One is the hardcore psychological reasons for making you do so. The other one has scientific and therapeutic reasons behind this exercise.

The psychological reason behind this exercise is to start getting experience from your day to day activities, which you are scared of. I mean such activities, which you are scared or fearful of, but those activities have least or no adverse impact if we go wrong doing those. The idea behind this chilled water exercise was to see how it feels after you do things, which you are scared of. I am sure that for most people, who will do this for the first time and stay there to observe their feelings in those moments, will have an eye-opening experience. You will realize that things which seem so scary, are less than half as bad, you keep on thinking.

Also, science has proved that having cold shower waters has lots of therapeutic benefits, which help you have sharper memory, improved courage, etc. A [2007 research study](https://www.ncbi.nlm.nih.gov/pubmed/17993252)[4] found that taking cold showers routinely can help treat depression symptoms often more effective than prescription medications. That's because

---

[4] https://www.ncbi.nlm.nih.gov/pubmed/17993252

cold water triggers a wave of mood-boosting neurochemicals which make you feel happy.

What else?

I know, you are feeling very excited now. Want some more?

Okay, take one more. It will not hit your body but disrupt your psychology for sure.

One example, which I found in the book titled "Flinch" by Julien Smith, you will find very absurd. But again, the idea is to test, how does it feel? I mean, you need to observe your feelings closely, while experimenting these. Only by observing those feelings, you will be armed with the necessary tools to kill your self-doubt. Because self doubt is nothing, but a feeling and emotion, which has solely arisen because of your thinking pattern in a specific way.

So, try this out. Please don't laugh. Honestly, I got surprised and laughed, when I read that first. But I gave it a try, and I request you to give it a try for sure, by keeping your rational mind aside for few moments.

Okay, here are the instructions!

- Go to your kitchen.
- Pick up a good glass or ceramic mug.
- Come out of your kitchen and in the middle of your living room or any other room, which has some open space.
- Now, stand there with that beautiful mug.
- The next step is to let that mug fall from the height of your head and onto the floor so that it breaks with a big noise. But before you throw the mug down, deeply observe and note your thoughts and feelings arising in your head. The rational thoughts could be like "you are crazy, or you have gone nuts, what will others

think about me, it seems silly." Also, there will be a feeling of a very little scare in your heart from your impending action.

- Okay, enough thinking and feeling, now simply drop that mug onto the floor. What happens? It turns into pieces with loud and screeching noise.
- Now check your feelings and emotions after this exercise. It is important to stand still for a moment and check out your feelings. How does it feel? There could be a feeling of a bit of amusement. You might laugh at yourself. Some might cry by seeing the rigidity of their mind getting softened.
- Just sit for some time, relaxed.

I urge you not to simply read this and feel like you have experimented. Your experiment will be your own experience; mine was only for mine. You are reading this book for changing your life, not for anybody else. Your self-doubts are in your head, so you need to trigger those emotions and feelings in your body and start to make the things move.

> *"All Life is an experiment, the more experiments you make the better"* ~ *Ralph Waldo Emerson*

So, the principle is "do it scared." The successful and confident people around the world are not born with such fearlessness. Rather what they do, is they do it despite being scared. They do it anyways.

Think about a person who is doing skydiving from 12000 feet up in the air from an airplane. Can you imagine what would be going on in the head and heart of that person the night before he has to jump in the morning?

You must watch this [YouTube video](https://www.youtube.com/watch?v=gG-F_rRVdLc)[5], to understand the feelings, which Will Smith, superstar of the movie **The Pursuit of Happyness**, explained having when he was doing this. The video explains this most hilariously, as the deepest fear of people. But it also explains what a feeling of relief and freedom is felt, once you go towards the other side of that fear. You open up a whole new world of opportunities in front of you.

Let me tell you, opportunities are always there in front of you. But you can't see them.

Why is it so?

Because the glasses you have worn are full of dust. The dust of fear and scare!

The only thing you have to do is to get the courage to remove these dirty glasses off your eyes. The world will be there to welcome you with the entire abundance. I

---

[5] https://www.youtube.com/watch?v=gG-F_rRVdLc

read a great another analogy from the best-selling book "Living Beyond Fear" by Zoe Mckey. Here is the excerpt, very beautifully told as final words from the author about how to look beyond your fear:

> *"If you have always looked downward, you haven't seen what lies ahead of you. If you put your palms in front of your eyes, you cover your sight. You can't see anything. However, if you slowly remove your palms from sight and put them in your pockets, they'll still be with you, but you won't focus on them. Now change the word "palms" to "fears." If you cover your sight because you let your fear dominate you, it will be very hard to see whatever good lies beneath.*
>
> *Are you ready to take away your "palms of fear" from your eyes? Fear*

is useful, and its message should be considered. However, your life should be about so much more than following your fears blindly."

John Lee Dumas, my virtual Mentor in the online business world (earning multi Million dollars per annum, in just five years of starting his podcast at www.eofire.com) says that he does at least one thing every week, which scares him like hell. So successful people choose to get scared while experimenting new things with their life.

How will doing this kill your self-doubts and improve your self-confidence?

These are small experiments to be done. But you have to start doing it in your day-to-day life gradually. The things like:

- Making a phone call to a client or customer, which you are scared about because you are delaying his deliverable.

- Going to your boss to ask for a raise in your salary.
- Raising your hand in your classroom in college to answer a question and you know everybody will look at you.
- Volunteering yourself to come on the stage to share some of your experience in front of hundreds of people.

You know, you will feel like what the heck, I am doing it. But I am telling you there is no other way. Yes, I said, no other way. No short -cut, my friend.

You have to start nipping your fears in the bud. By staying with your fear is like feeding a monster, which will someday become so big that it will swallow you. Don't feed your fear. Rather feed your courage muscle. Make your courage stronger, and it will serve you big time. It will win you your life.

Don't worry about initial failures while trying something new. Don't ever take initial failures as setbacks and start thinking your fear was right.

Use the phrase "**I have failed this time**" rather than thinking "I **am the failure.**"

> *"Never be ashamed of a scar. It simply means you were stronger than whatever tried to hurt you" ~ Unknown*

Ryan Holiday, in his book, "Obstacle is the Way." States that fear and failures appear like obstacles in your way. But in fact, these are the testing instruments put in your way to check if you have the necessary ingredients in yourself to attain success.

7. Start with End in Mind

Imagine any of your specific goals, which you want to achieve in a given amount of time. It could be related to your finances, your work, your relationships, your personal and spiritual life or anything which you care about.

Now, you have identified a particular goal and wanted to figure out where to start, what action to take. Also, you start realizing the obstacles coming on the way. Attaining every goal is nothing but a journey from point A to point B.

Imagine you have entered into a new modern residential township to meet one of your friends there. You know the block and flat number of your friend, but you don't know the way to reach there. Now you see a guiding map put on the street side. There is a big red dot in the middle of the map, which says "You are Here." Immediately, the next thing is, you start locating your destination on the map. Once located, now you look at the street numbers or the directions to follow from your current location to the destination. You also see, how far to go straight and then where to take a left or a right turn. You also find for some key landmark place on the way, for example, some supermarket or some school, college or anything which is easily identifiable. Because you want to be sure and keep track that you are going in the right direction. These are signposts which lead you to your ultimate destination, i.e., your friends' house.

So, what do you get from this example?

You started keeping your focus on end, in your mind. You located your destination, then found the directions. You also took the pain to notice and locate various landmark as your relevant milestones, to ensure that you are on the right path. The same we all need to do with our life goals.

But you would say there is a problem. God has not given us a clear roadmap to exactly reach the destination. I would go one step further and say that not only this, there is one bigger problem.

Guess What?

God has also not earmarked for us any dreams or pursuits to be followed by us. Such a funny situation, you know. You are not provided with the roadmap showing from where to start, and more strangely, you have not been provided with any destination as well.

What do you do?

Here is the thing. Pay attention to it. God has given us the consciousness, which is given only to the human beings, as a special feature. Moreover, don't think that by not giving you the roadmap or destination, He has done something bad to you. Rather, think about it differently. He has kept the whole universe open to you. You have just to have to become intentional and keep your finger on it, and that thing becomes your destination, your own chosen goal, not imposed upon you by God. You choose the destination on your own. You can opt for the moon, or you simply limit yourself to just a few steps away. Totally, yourchoice!

You have got your destination so now one problem is solved. But another one still remains as it is? Is there any roadmap which can guide you on your journey so that you can start with the end in mind?

The answer to that is "Just look around."

Whatever you wish to do, there are enough chances that there are people who would have done that already. I follow below quote, which is a gem, so often whenever I am in a state of doubt.

> ***"Success leaves Clues"***
> *~ Tony Robbins*

There are footprints of people who have traveled that path and they are more than willing to help you find out the way and even hold your hand. If you would have thought a few decades ago about traveling in space, you might have had difficulty finding answers. Today, even that has been done by man, and you can even touch and feel space now.

Whatever you intend to attain, you are just away by typing few words on google. You will definitely find relevant information in the form of some article, course or any other information material, which can help you guide the way. At the least, you will be able to find some leading material, which you can explore further to reach towards your solutions.

This book is prepared on this very principle, i.e., start with the end in mind. The way this book was started is as follows.

I kept the end goal in my mind, which was that this book will be read by a reader Avatar, who is either suffering badly from self-doubt or it might be that he wants to overcome even minor instances of self doubts totally. I am targeting the readers who would connect with my way of explanation, examples, the success stories, stories told by me (basis my research) and then the solutions offered. Also, my objective is that the person reading this book immediately starts moving and taking action after reading each chapter. I wanted this book to give the real actionable strategies without fluffing it too much with theories. With that goal in mind, I already decided the exact necessary elements to be captured in this book. I worked on the outline of the book with those necessary points. Only after that, I started writing chapter after chapter. Now I know the end destination, and I also know the roadmap after writing half a dozen books already.

You know, knowing the end before you start is something which keeps your "Motivation lamp" lighted. It keeps guiding you to a particular place at the required pace.

So whatever obstacles come in your way, while moving towards the end results, you just need to remember the principles stated in another chapter of the book guiding you to take action, despite being scared.

> ***"If you have no***
> ***destination in mind,***

> ***you will never get there" ~ Harvey Mackey***

Okay, enough for this chapter. Let's move on to the next one now.

8. Action is Your Master Key

I believe in the Hindu religion. One of the sacred books of Hindus is "Geeta." This book is counted as a religious book, but great people have also coined this as Life Book because it teaches you practically the life lessons in each area of life.

Geeta is a compilation of sermons, which Lord Krishna has imparted to Arjuna, who got deeply immersed in negative thinking and was so plagued that he was not willing to take any action. He wanted to run away from the battlefield and in a sense from life itself. So, Lord Krishna has imparted the priceless teachings to him, which are covered in this book. The most important teaching, which if one wants to pick up, not merely intellectually, but also applying it practically, will make you so aware that you would get answers to most of your problems in life.

But the irony is that we don't understand the plain one-liners. We need tons of information to understand the simplest things of life, but we hardly apply those things practically. Let me tell you very frankly, if more information is the resolution, the world would have already become a heaven with no problems therein at all. Some report suggests that Amazon itself has more than 5 million books listed there, and hundreds of thousands of books are added to that every year.

But man keeps on reading, reading, and more reading, but still not finding the answers to his quests.

I was reading, not sure where, but very much relevant, regarding learning vs. practical implementation. There is some study that if you want the medical/health benefits of consuming turmeric, you must ALSO consume a little black pepper with it.

It's like 5% effective when you take turmeric alone. But It's 100% effective if you add the black pepper into it.

Similarly, Learning is just 5%, but learning and then DOING is 100%.

Let's come to the teachings of Geeta. It will sound obvious and a matter of common sense. But you all know well that common sense is not a common practice.

Geeta's shloka (teaching) from the relevant chapter as translated in English is as follows.

> ***"A person has the right***
> ***towards action alone***
> ***and not towards the***
> ***fruit of action. Let not***
> ***the fruit of action be***
> ***the motive for acting.***
> ***Also, let there not be***

> *any attachment to inaction."*

You have to focus on your actions solely and not worry about the outcome. Of course, you have to be clear about the end goal and take actions to achieve that end goal. But the key lesson here is that while taking action, you should not consistently be anxious or worried about the results.

There could be only two kinds of results arising from your actions. One, you succeed, and another is you don't succeed. In fact, both the results are helpful. If you succeed, that is your goal, so celebrate. If you don't, then it gives you lessons, which you have to learn and implement to make it a success.

> *"Failure doesn't mean the game is over. It means try again with*

> ***experience" ~ Len Schlesinger***

Edison would have also been frustrated about 1000 failures while trying to invent the light bulb. But he got success only after 1000 attempts. His wording was that those 1000 attempts were not failures, rather these were the lessons that these things don't work, and you have to try a different approach. When a reporter asked, "How did it feel to fail **1,000 times**?" **Edison** replied, "I didn't fail **1,000 times**. The **light bulb** was an invention with **1,000** steps."

But my friend, I assume that you are not going to do any world-record breaking invention, to disrupt the world. I took the liberty to have this assumption because you wouldn't have been reading this book, if you had been already on that path (meaning you would have crossed that stage of self-doubt already). You know your end goal, and you know the actions to be taken, so what you need to do is to keep taking action without worrying about the results.

You have to be persistent in pursuing your goal. While pursuing that goal, your life may take different directions, who knows, life will put different opportunities in front of you, which you would have never imagined ever.

> ***"Stay committed to your decisions. But stay flexible in your approach" ~ Tony Robbins***

There are enough examples in history, where people changed their entire career and took altogether different paths in their lives. Whatever you do in your life, keep doing with the full faith and without worrying too much about future.

The best-selling author and high-performance strategist Robin Sharma was a litigation lawyer before he took the bold decision to quit his profession and started an altogether different path of inspiring the world. He self-published his book and started his journey to inspire the world. He wouldn't have ever thought of such an amazing journey while starting a career as a lawyer. Life can throw ample opportunities in front of you, provided you keep taking consistent action.

Don't get engrossed in self doubt, by the intermittent failures coming in the way. They are in fact, the stepping stones for your success in life.

Either way, you are going to be succeeding. Either you will succeed in your own desired goals, or else you will learn and succeed next time. And it might happen that you are showered upon a different life path altogether, which you would have neither dreamed of ever.

Keep taking action and let's move to the next chapter now.

9. Use Lack of Knowledge as Positive Trigger

One of the biggest reasons why you doubt yourself and your capabilities is because you think that you lack the necessary knowledge and skill-sets necessary to accomplish your goal or finish that task. Have you ever tried to go deeper into your mind and examine what this doubt indicates?

Get ready; my below statement probably might hurt you. And I am not going to say sorry because I want to give you some shock treatment therapy.

I am bluntly saying that you are cooking up a false story here. This is the excuse you are smartly selling to yourself for not taking action. You are not willing to take responsibility. Or simply speaking, you don't want it so badly yet. This is nothing but cheating your own conscience.

By making such lame excuses, you are simply saying that others who have done it or reached there, got this knowledge from the womb of their mothers. You say that Bill Gates was by birth knowing the computer coding and he simply created windows by that knowledge. Do you think he didn't put out any effort to learn the newer things? Forget about that time, when he was on the journey of creating an empire, look at him today. You will be surprised to see his urge to learn, even at this stage, when most will wonder why would he need to learn anything further. Just check out his blog www.gatesnotes.com, and you will be shocked to see what kind of books he continues to read. You would notice the versatility of the topics he keeps on learning and sharing with the world. Just leave this book for a moment here and click on the link above to see, what Bill is up to (before you skip this). Below quote aptly applies to him:

> *"Today a Reader,*
> *Tomorrow a Leader"* ~
> *Margaret Fuller*

You think that Oprah Winfrey, an African American media personality (net worth > 3 Billion USD), was charismatic by birth and she just went ahead and started her Opera Winfrey Show, which is one of the highest-rated television talk show in American Television History. Do you think that she succeeded without being required to learn anything new? My friend, just check out her life story! You will be shocked to know what a tragic childhood she had, with an abusive parent, getting raped at eight years and being pregnant in her teens and still she not only survived but came out thriving in the life. Look at this video https://www.youtube.com/watch?v=-

knvvSja7Ac and you will bow your head in front of her. I insist you watch this video to know the power of stronger inner motivation to learn and change your destiny, from whatever background you had.

Do you know Tim Ferriss? He is an American author, entrepreneur, self-proclaimed "human guinea pig", and public speaker, who got famous with best seller book "The 4-Hour Workweek: Escape 9-5, Live Anywhere, and Join the New Rich". (I openly admit, this book has inspired me to think in an unconventional manner and introduced me to this whole new world of online business and now becoming an author-preneur- and I am really grateful that I read that book) was about to commit suicide in his early days due to depression and self-doubt on what to do next in his life. Fortunately, his relatives tracked that he had bought a book or material titled something like "how to commit suicide without pain."

This is what he has officially admitted in one of his podcasts. Now check him out, coming out with one after another best seller, his latest being "[Tools of Titans: The Tactics, Routines, and Habits of Billionaires, Icons, and World-Class Performers](). He is considered amongst the most sought after disruptive thought leaders of the world. Check him out at his blog https://tim.blog/.

Look at the people who have reached the stage of committing suicide, how much self-doubt they would have had in their minds about their lives. Thinking of committing suicide means that one is left without any self-confidence and no purpose in life. These people even doubt their very existence on this planet. This is the height of self doubt, isn't it?

But the lesson which you can take out of their stories is that they had come out of that phase and went ahead to learn and master knowledge and are thriving now. I sincerely hope that none of my readers who are reading this book should ever think of going that far on the wrong road. After learning the life story of the above people, you can't even make that excuse that they are some super human. You now already know the phases, when they were at the extreme lowest point in their lives. So, there is a ray of hope. It only requires one thing. Commit to learning. Be a life-long learner.

If you are committed enough to learn, then you will surely find the ways.

In this modern world, you can't make a fool of yourself for stating lack of resources, even if you wish to. Let me put it very frankly. If you are reading this book on the Kindle or your smartphone or even if you are reading it on the paperback (ordered through online payment), it demonstrates that you are living in a country where you have electricity, internet, bank account, smartphone, etc. You are already part of the civilized population, which is blessed with these life-changing amenities. With all these things, no one can even imagine that you don't know world's "go to place." Google.

I guess you already understood my point beyond doubt. But still, I will make it bold and clear.

You can learn anything if you wish to. You can even fly an airplane in the case of emergency, i.e., when all the pilots in the plane have got a sudden severe stomach ache or something like that. You just need to open a YouTube video and type how to fly an airplane and you got the lecture in front of you. I just searched on Google and found 94 million web pages teaching you that. See this YouTube video: https://www.youtube.com/watch?v=cGgzAhpTgvs . Don't think I am making fun.

Everything is practically possible, and yes, God forbid, if you are ever in any such emergency, be resourceful and use the tools at your fingertips.

So, the point is very clear that you can learn anything you want. There are also structured online courses available on all topics on different platforms. Check out www.udemy.com, an online platform to learn the stuff at dirt low prices and the quality is also good. I have personally tried a few things. Besides Udemy, just check out www.mooc-list.com, you will find the detailed list of all the online courses available on the internet. MOOC stands for Massive Open Online Courses if you wish to know.

So, now the availability barrier is totally gone, everything is available to you at free of cost or dirt low prices, if wish to learn.

But how to use the lack of knowledge as your trigger point?

I deliberately made the previous section full of certain examples to put the point across, so that you can convince your mind that lack of knowledge is really not a reason to stop moving ahead.

Now, I will tell you how you can make your lack of knowledge the trigger point to your ultimate success. Remember, I explained in the previous chapter about starting with the end in mind. Now to reach a particular destination or achievement, you may realize that there is some lack of skill or knowledge, which will become a hurdle to your success. You are so willing to attain that objective, but this lack of knowledge is posing a threat against you. So, what do you do?

You should make this hurdle as you trigger point. But trigger for what?

This assessment of lack of knowledge will work in two wonderful ways. First, it will immediately give you the action step, i.e., you have to look for the resources and learn that in the shortest possible time. This will in itself pave your way for working towards your goal. Secondly, and which is most important, is that you will never doubt yourself again in your lifetime for lack of knowledge because you have already experienced that you can learn anything and apply the same to the real-life situation, if you are really motivated enough to do that.

Use learning as a vehicle to conquer all your self-doubts and accelerate your pace towards achieving your goals.

> *"The more you learn,*
> *the more you earn"* ~
> *Warren Buffet*

10. Never Blame Again

"What the heck should I do when there is someone out there, who is really responsible for the mess created," you would scream, right?

This would be an obvious reaction, after reading the chapter title, from most of the readers. Because this is the way, we have been brought up. This is what we see around us. Everyone starts blaming others for whatever happens in their lives. Our fingers are always pointed to others if something goes wrong.

You must be familiar with these below sentences, which you hear more often around you. Might be that, you speak this language to yourself sometimes or more often.

a. What is my fault, if there was traffic on the way and I got late for the meeting because of that?
b. Had my colleague delivered the work in time, I would have finished the project earlier.
c. My parents didn't provide the right upbringing or the decent education, so I can't progress anymore.
d. My spouse doesn't understand my feelings or doesn't carry the same values, as I do, so I don't feel like I should pursue my true passion.
e. I got in an accident, and there was no fault of mine, so why I am being punished for that.
f. Nobody has ever done that crazy new venture in my family and surroundings, and they won't understand what I am doing, so better live as per my society standard and not try anything new.

The list can go on and on.

There can always be some reasons outside of you, which have turned things adversely for you. Also, there may not be any fault of you at all for such mishaps or accident or whatever goof up has happened in your days or life in general. But, the most important question here is that what the next course of action should be.

What do you do now?

Would you just blame the others and stop there, doing nothing? Or would you take a different approach and start thinking, how can I make the best out of the current situation?

> *"It's not what happens to you that determines how far you will go in life; it is how you handle what happens to you"* ~ *Zig Ziglar*

You have to take responsibility for your next best action.

I am not saying that you don't have to tell others if they are doing something wrong. You must tell them they are accountable for what they do. If someone has put his or her shoe on your foot and it is hurting you, you don't need to stand there like a fool. You have to tell him or her to remove his or her shoe. Suppose your colleague has delayed the delivery of work in given time. Now, you are under tremendous pressure to meet the deadlines. It is a clear example, where you weren't at any fault, but you have to bear the burden for his or her fault.

So, what would you do now?

There could be two possible reactions from anyone in this scenario.

The first alternative, which people mostly adopt, is like this. You will put the blame on your colleague and don't take any steps to improve the situation to complete the deadline, somehow. You doubt your capability to meet the deadline or you now have got the excuse not to do the work.

The second alternative goes differently. You very categorically tell your colleague that he or she is responsible for the delay from the agreed timelines. You make him or her accountable for his or her delay and him or her realize that they would be responsible for the consequences of their default. Next thing you do is to stop the blame game. You don't doubt your capability; rather you buckle down and put sincere efforts to recover from the situation and bring the best out of it. You will find the ways to mitigate the damage. Maybe you request your superiors to give you additional support for few days to give the best shot to finish the project in time.

You see the difference in both approaches. The first one is victim's approach, in which you put the blame on others and even start shrugging off from your responsibility. The second approach is taking hold in the driver's seat and taking the things forward despite whatever wrong has already happened.

Zig Ziglar, one of the best motivational speaker of the modern era, in his conference had shared one of his personal examples of taking the responsibility in a difficult situation. He was working with a direct sales company selling cookware. In his 20s, he was offered to head the sales operations of one of the big regions of his company in the United States. This was because the existing regional head was not able to run the operations profitably. Moreover, Zig has shown some good results in selling skills at his young age.

Zig was happy to get this enhanced responsibility. But suddenly, things started falling apart. His immediate would-be subordinate was diagnosed with some disease, and he had to go for some treatment. Another key employee, who had to support Zig in taking charge over the new responsibility, somehow got another opportunity and he moved on from the company. And there were some other problems which had led to a reduction in the sales of the company already. All in all, he was in such a situation that there was no fault of his, but things started appearing unappealing to him. Even he felt himself dwarf before the situation and started blaming the outside situation as a reason for not being able to handle the region well.

But, He was Zig, you know. He sensed that his instant behavior or reaction to the situation was not up to the mark. He picked up a great book titled "The Power of Positive

<u>Thinking</u>" by Norman Vincent Peale. He read the complete book in short time. Now there was a total change in his attitude and approach to handling the situation. He realized that of course, the situation was bad and moreover, he didn't play any role at all in making the conditions worse. But he told himself that whatever the case may be. he had to take the responsibility and turn things around, even in the given scenario.

So, he made up the plans, and immediately hired the right set of people. He himself traveled extensively to different sales locations. And finally, not only he was able to improve the sales of that region, rather his unit got the second position across the United States in selling the products in very short period.

Isn't the message quite clear here? Therefore, even if you are not at any fault, you still have to take responsibility for improving the situation.

There are tons of examples around, where brave people have taken charge of their lives, despite the negative circumstances around them, without making an excuse or doubting their capabilities.

Arunima Sinha, an Indian athlete, is a live example of taking responsibility for her life. Life didn't play a fair game with her. She was planning to be a mountaineer and was going for some training to some location in a train. In that train, there were some robbers, who tried to rob her of her gold chain. But she was a sports person and didn't give up easily. She resisted the efforts of robbers to snatch her gold chain, but had to pay a huge cost. She was thrown off the moving train. The worst part, when the robbers threw her off the train, there was another train passing at the next track. Though she survived the accident, her both legs were amputated. She was lying in the hospital bed with relatives pouring in. Her sole dream of being a mountaineer seemingly had died without her legs.

For a moment, imagine yourself in that situation. What would you do? 99.99% would play the victim's role and give up by blaming the circumstances around. But she didn't let the self-doubt engulf her anymore. She determined to climb the Mount Everest with artificial legs. People mocked at her decision, marking that as being an insane step. But she was determined and took responsibility for taking the next best action. The rest is history. She did raise the India flag on Mount Everest in the year 2013 and was also given the Padma Shree Award by the President of India. I had the privilege of meeting her at one event, where she was the speaker telling her bravery journey. If you wish, you can read her complete story at https://yourstory.com/2015/05/arunima-sinha-world-champion/

These above stories are nothing but a way to show you that there are people who have taken responsibility for their life and life has rewarded them immensely from all perspectives. They had much better reasons to blame the circumstances than most of the population around (which has false self-doubts in their heads only).

So, don't skip living your life, merely by minor disturbances coming in your way. Don't let yourself start doubting yourself or blaming others. Rather take charge of the situation, and in no time, you will start seeing yourself as conquering your self-doubts and crossing the new frontiers.

> ***"Discontent, blaming, complaining, self-pity cannot serve as a foundation for a good***

future, no matter how much effort you make"
~ Echarte Tolle

---

11. Seek Help relentlessly

It is often the case with most people that they keep getting mad in their own heads, by just repeating their self-doubts and wrong beliefs again and again. But what is the benefit of repeating such thoughts? Do they help? No, they don't, rather they aggravate the problem.

The best approach is to just get out of your head. Get out of your place and seek help, if you have any doubt about anything. You can never get a different perspective on the one thing that you have been thinking for the hundredth time. You should approach some third person you consider to be wiser and more experienced about the problem you are seeking the answers to. That person will be able to objjectively assess the thoughts ongoing in your mind. It is only an outside third person, who can give you honest feedback about the right or wrong direction of your thoughts and can help guide you in taking some further action.

You may have started thinking that you are not good enough in certain areas of your work or some other specific aspect. You might be thinking of giving up in that area, affected by this self doubt. Now, instead of allowing this thought to settle in your brain, you need to simply go out and check out with your friends or family, who you consider mature enough to handle this. They might be able to tell you the quick resources which you can utilize and develop your skills in that area.

Everyone Needs Help

Don't overthink in your mind that by seeking help from someone, you would become smaller than the other person. Rather it is the other way around. Successful people seek help more than often from others; rather it is the exchange of help, i.e., they help each other.

Look at the top business schools, engineering or law school graduates. They stay in close touch with the alumni groups from their institutions and keep discussing with each other about the better work opportunities. They also continue to learn from each other about the latest developments and best practices to sharpen their skills. Because they believe in the below:

> ***"It is not what you know; it is who do you know" ~ Proverb***

By your knowledge, you have limitations of finite amount of time with you, i.e., you only have 24 hours in a day. You can learn on your own only as much as the limited time you have. But if you know tons of other people in your trade or craft, then you compound the effect of your learning. This is because everybody is learning, while you are learning. If you have ten people around you, who you can approach, you have 10X learning and knowledge with you. By this principle, you can easily 100X your knowledge and learning.

Seeking help psychologically is also very soothing. You feel much more connected to the other person if you can get help from the other person. There is a feeling of deeper gratitude and bonding with the other person.

Let's admit. You don't have all the answers on this planet. No one has. So better, instead of getting locked in your own cocoon, look outside your small world and seek help from others. In fact, no one can do it all alone.

The business world is like a football match. You have to pass the ball often and also take the ball from others as a team to move in the right direction and pace to hit the goal. Every player in the team has a different skill set and strength. No one is less important because each has a role to play in the bigger goal. This example may better fit about the teamwork. But the central theme is that you have to seek the help of others to achieve your goals faster. If you are seeking help from someone, you might have some kind of strength or skill set, which you can offer in return to the other person.

You would notice, the more successful a person is, more well-connected he would be. In fact, there is a concept of masterminding, where people brainstorm ideas with each other and offer help to each other for mutual growth.

> ***"If I have seen further than others, it is by standing upon the shoulders of giants"***
> ***~Isaac Newton***

But why don't you ask for help?

Who stops you?

In fact, no one from outside! It is only your own small organ of 3 pounds lying in between your two ears. Yes, your own mind is the real obstacle in seeking out help for various reasons.

Before seeking help, you think in your own head, as to what another person will think about me. You get scared that the other person might think that you are so naive or stupid that you don't know even such a small thing. Some of you might have a very strong ego. You think that why should you go to someone else for any kind of help or support? . Approaching someone else for seeking help seems a direct attack on your own ego.

Another reason why you don't seek help is you might over-think that the other person would be too busy to offer you any help. You think that seeking help would be disturbing the other person, so you better stay getting deeper and deeper into your problem.

But, you know one thing which I have realized; that people who reach the top (generally who travel the journey from deep low to super high in success) really understand the pain of the persons just starting or traveling behind. They understand the difficulties or challenges of the initial days, they faced in their own lives and which could be avoided by having some minor tweaks in the approach towards the problem.

But they will not come to know on their own that you have some problem, nor will they travel far, come to you and knock your door to offer help to you. You have to approach them politely and precisely seek the required help, after doing the requisite research on your part. If your problem is such that a simple google search can help, then don't expect wasting the time of others on such things. But if you have done enough homework and have jotted down the precise areas of concerns, others will appreciate your sincere efforts and would be more than happy to help.

It is not simply a theory, rather, I have personally implemented this and have successfully avoided some pitfalls or moved a few steps ahead faster. In his book, "13 Steps to Bloody Good Luck", Ashwin Sanghi, the author, has put this approach of taking the courage to approach other people as one of the best ways to invite luck towards you.

Collaboration is the key

The modern age is an age of collaboration. You will see many thought leaders joining hands with each other and promoting each other's works on different platforms. Seeking help from the people who have already reached their goal definitely helps. If you have some product to sell or services to offer, which complement others' offerings, they would be very happy to promote your work. Or if you have some query on any of your professional topics, you can bury your head in the books for hours to find the answers. But the shorter way is, of course, to call up few of your acquaintances or friends, who have already been in that field and would have done it and there are much better chances that you will get quicker answers.

I give a personal example related to my previous book "Focus Mastery," I reached out to one of my author friends, who also writes in the personal growth niche. I checked with her if she liked the book and would be willing to let her subscribers know about it. She happily agreed to shoot an email to her email subscribers apprising them about my book. And this gave me an instant boost invisibility of my book and also the book touched the Amazon bestseller #1 rank.

What did it cost to me? Nothing, just a simple email request.

Therefore, don't limit yourself to be guided by your own limited mind. Don't drown yourself in the self doubt about your insufficient knowledge or lack of competency or skill set. You only need a positive frame of mind and should openly reach out to people to seek help. Rather you should approach as many people outside as you can, to seek guidance on different aspects. Also, it goes without saying that you have to be helpful to them in exchange, too.

> *"You can get everything in life you want if you will just help enough other people get what they want"~ Zig Ziglar*

---

12. Be Your Own Thought Commando.

Garbage in Garbage Out

You must be familiar with this concept about computer science. Garbage In, Garbage Out (GIGO) is where flawed, or nonsense input data produces nonsense output or "garbage." It means, if you put useless data in the computer, it will not give you the best of results.

Your mind is also like a computer. There are estimates that every day our minds run around 60000 thoughts, and more than 95% of them are a mere repetition of the previously run thoughts already.

So, whatever thoughts, you are thinking, if those are bad quality thoughts, these will impact your outer action. Your thoughts are the inputs to your mind, which in turn generates different emotions and these lead to you feeling in a certain way. And based on basis that feeling, you take action or don't take any action at all.

Suppose you allow a negative thinking to run in your mind that person X had done bad things to you and you should take revenge upon him. You can easily guess what kind of emotions and feelings, such thoughts will generate. Obviously, you will have negative feelings and emotions, which will prompt you to devise strategies to cause some damage or loss to that person.

But you have the power to switch that thought with another one like, "The person has done something bad with me, I already had tough communication with him or her. Now I have learned a lesson never to deal with him again. I will now focus on my other life priorities." What results will such thoughts bring to your life? Of course, you will be focused on the important things in your life, rather than waste time in taking revenge.

Do you see the difference between the two thoughts? The first one was garbage and the second one was gold. And all this is the cause and effect principle playing its role, meaning your thoughts are the cause and your actions are the effect of your thoughts. If you want to change the effect or the outcome, you first have to change the cause.

So, Be Your Thought Commando?

Assume yourself as a Commando, whose role is to never allow any wrong people inside the gate of your coveted master. You know that any wrong people can cause damage to the master, so you stand armed with your weapons and full strength to keep such people outside your gate.

Now, ask this commando also to guard yourself from the negative thoughts. Because, you know that any negative thoughts will badly affect you, so you want to stop them at your gate. Ask a simple question, whenever any thoughts come to your head. "Does this thought serve me or else destroy me?" Allow only those thoughts, which are helpful towards your life goals and scrap all others at the gate.

Don't worry; you won't get bored, rather observing your thoughts is going to be an interesting game. This will improve your mindfulness and concentration if you can categorize your thoughts in these two buckets of helpful thoughts and destroying thoughts. The success is nothing but being able to mark the distinction between what is bad for you (so that you skip that) and what is good for you (so that you can do more of that). By this exercise, in very short period, you will be able to remove the negative effects of self-doubt and empower yourself with the positive thoughts.

It can be compared to a glass of muddy water. How will you clean the muddy water? The simplest solution is to keep pouring the clean water onto the glass. You will see the muddy water going out of the glass, as you keep putting the clean water in the glass. As the quantity of cleaner water gets more and more in the glass, the water starts getting clear. In no time, you will be able to see the glass with transparent water, which you can see through.

Similarly, if you can fill your mind with all positive and actionable thoughts, you will shortly be able to see much more clearly. You will be better able to look at the opportunities and grab them for your benefits.

What allows the good thoughts?

If you don't invite or affirmatively call for the good thoughts, they don't come on their own. The mind is generally a frightful creature by its nature. It only can think of survival and to stay safe from any danger, so it will produce thoughts, which will help you to remain in your safety zone. It will not produce the positive thoughts on its own.

Surround yourself with great literature, which prompts you towards the betterment of your life. Don't watch TV and merely look for your entertainment or watch news only. They don't serve you for a better future. Use the internet to search the areas of development and improve your areas of learning.

Don't waste too much time on entertainment, rather provide for your education, which will help you to overcome your negative thoughts and self-doubts, make you more resourceful and prime you for taking fast and effective action.

13. Create Your New Surround System

> *"You are the average of five people, you spend most time with"*
> *~ Jim Rohn*

What are you made of?

Your body is made up by the food you eat, and your mind is made up of thoughts, which you regularly think of. Where do your thoughts come from? Your surrounding environment prompts your thoughts. Whatever you are today is because of the atmosphere around you. You have borrowed all the belief systems from your society.

This is good news in fact. This makes the solution to your self-doubt problem much easier. If your present is made up of the thoughts you have so far, as a result of your surrounding environment, you have only a simple action to perform for a better future.

I repeat the above in a bit different manner because this statement is so important that it needs stronger emphasis. Your present situation is all due to your environment and belief system, which you have been in for a long time. Therefore, if you want to see your future to be in an altogether positive direction, you have to change your environment.

Consider a child, who is born in a developing country with lack of resources. Send him for six months to a developed country like the United States and provide him a healthy environment with friends and education. You can imagine the changes in the child after that short period. He will grasp the new language from the environment. The child will groom quickly. It is the same child, who if had to stay in the developing country would have a different approach towards life, but a healthy environment will change his perspective and approach towards life.

That's the reason, successful people cautiously hang out with only successful people. You won't see any successful entrepreneurs, or professionals hanging out with the paupers. They choose, rather they sincerely craft their environment in a way, which can help them to nurture their minds for a better future.

You need to have a revisit on your association of people or network.

Have a sincere look at the environment around you. How many people are involved in making your environment? Simply put, you will have a family, If a bachelor, you are staying with parents or if married, you are staying with spouse and kids. For work, either you are an employee or work on your own, so you have the colleagues in the office or the clients or customers your deal with. For weekends, you will have a network of friends or relatives, with whom you plan to hang out and spend time with.

Let's take it one by one.

Family comes first. The family is the most important aspect of anyone's life, and one spends the most time with, after one's work hours. These people love you and come in the category of your well-wishers. But you have to check the definition of your well-wisher in the initial chapter of the book. If you don't recollect, go back to the chapter and have a relook to refresh your concept.

If they don't fit into the category of well-wisher, then you can't immediately change them, unlike your job or your friends, where it is easy to make changes much faster. So, let's be clear. You can't change your spouse as quickly, as you can your friends. At least, in India, where I live, this concept is not looked at very positively, unlike the western part of the globe, where people part their ways, if there is a mismatch in the thought process or approach towards the life. I personally advocate that one should try best to maintain as cordial relations with the family as possible.

The best way to deal with the negativity from family members is trying to dilute their negativity. You can make them meet with your positive thinking friends or colleagues. As this will change their environment and it might positively impact their thinking, as they would would hear the thoughts from different sources, not you, which they consider as an old radio station playing the same old songs.

Also, one of the best pieces of advice for dealing with such persons is never try to win any arguments with them. Firstly, you won't win, and second, even if you win, you will lose a lot like your peace of mind, your optimism. So be disciplined with your cravings to ever argue with them. Be polite and firm in your stand, though.

Now, look at your office colleagues and friends circle. If you think that being with them doesn't enhance your quality of life, rather you get some negative feelings about your work or life in general, then it is the time to re-think. You need to subtly start making the distance from these people and start building the new network of people, which can uplift our life.

In my previous book "Master You Day Design Your Life," I have a dedicated chapter on how to deal with negative people in your environment. I have divided these persons into two categories "Mandatory Negative Partners" and "Optional Negative Partners" Then the chapter goes on to explain a number of ways to deal with each such category, with effective strategies. If you are interested, you may check that out at above link or by searching with book name at Amazon.com.

Surround yourself with Achievers:

While you have to stay away from all kinds of negative people, you need to take specific action to make new friends, which will help you to grow your life. Brendon Burchard, in his book "[The Charge: Activating the 10 Human Drives That Make You Feel Alive](#)" calls such people growth friends. He even recommends that you should have ten such friends, who will uplift your game in all facets of life.

Finding such people in the short run may be a bit challenging. But you can go to different seminars, conferences of your interest and offer your hand to shake often. Who knows, your best partners could be hanging out at such places? Physical contact is the best possible thing you can have in terms of networking. This is because you can meet them, see them, feel their emotions and get benefitted from their vibrations. There are various ways to reach out to people.

One of the best ways I have explored is www.meetup.com, which is an online platform, where people can create groups and meet each other physically. I have attended multiple such groups ranging from simple Coffee Meet-up, Silence and Meditation meet-up, to start up/entrepreneurship Meet-up. It is really a good platform to connect with like-minded people for sure. Now I am looking for some authors and readers meet-up group to learn and share the lessons in the thought leadership industry.

Also, you should look out for events being organized in your town or nearby. It is worthwhile to spend few bucks to go there, to learn the new content and also to meet new people. Just Google and you will find a number of events happening in or around your town.

The online platform is the quickest platform to connect virtually. I never undermine the importance of online connections. You may not have met them physically, but you can relate to them and share your thoughts with them on social media, etc. Also, it is not necessary to have the two-way connection with people. What I mean is you should follow the industry leaders and learn from them. They may not know you, but you should follow their work and the content they share online this will help you to deprive your mind of all kind of negativity and self doubt.

Your new positive environment will give you confidence and courage to look at the life differently.

> *"The Richest persons in the world look for and build networks; everyone else looks for work"* ~ *Robert T. Kiyosaki*

Final Words...

"Every good thing comes to an end, but always consider the end as a beginning of new chapter of your life" ~ Anonymous

---

This brings me to the end of this book.

As I said, in the beginning, you don't need tons of tactics; you merely need a change in your psychology and mindset to look at things in your life with a different perspective.

I have started this book with a special emphasis on the preparation to be done to develop your mindset. Once you are equipped with positive psychology and coachable mindset, the strategies and tactics presented in this book will be your second nature in no time.

I have personally benefitted a ton from these simple mental tweaks and some outside changes. I am quite convinced that if you apply these tactics, you will start seeing improvements in your life in the next few weeks. As you know, knowledge is power, but implement is the key.

I wish you a life beyond self-doubt, which is a life full of self-confidence and freedom. So, go ahead and start taking action today onwards.

I want you to say this quote to yourself loud enough and start your new journey.

> ***"Today I close the door***
> ***to the past, open the***
> ***new door to the future,***

take a deep breath, step on through and start a new chapter in my life."

******

Your Free Gift Bundle:

Did you download your Gift Bundle already?

Click and Download your Free Gift Bundle Below

You can also grab your FREE GIFT BUNDLE through this below URL:

http://sombathla.com/freegiftbundle

Copyright © 2017 by Som Bathla

All rights reserved. No part of this book may be reproduced in any form without permission in writing from the author.

DISCLAIMER

No part of this publication may be reproduced or transmitted in any form or by any means, mechanical or electronic, including photocopying or recording, or by any information storage and retrieval system, or transmitted by email without permission in writing from the author.

While all attempts have been made to verify the information provided in this publication, the author does not assume any responsibility for errors, omissions, or contrary interpretations of the subject matter herein.

The views expressed are those of the author alone, and should not be taken as expert instruction or commands. The reader is responsible for his or her own actions.

Adherence to all applicable laws and regulations, including international, federal, state, and local governing professional licensing, business practices, advertising, and all other aspects of doing business in any jurisdiction in the world is the sole responsibility of the purchaser or reader.

www.ingramcontent.com/pod-product-compliance
Lightning Source LLC
Chambersburg PA
CBHW020646220526
45464CB00001B/312